Growing Through Conflict

Growing Through Conflict

ERWIN LUTZER

SERVANT PUBLICATIONS
ANN ARBOR, MICHIGAN

Vine Books is an imprint of Servant Publications especially designed to serve evangelical Christians.

Unless otherwise noted, all Scripture references are from the *New American Standard Bible,* © the Lockman Foundation 1960, 1962, 1963, 1968, 1971, 1972, 1973, 1975, 1977; other references are from the *Authorized King James Version* (KJV).

Published by Servant Publications
P.O. Box 8617
Ann Arbor, Michigan 48107

Cover design by Paul Higdon, Minneapolis, Minn.

01 02 03 04 10 9 8 7 6 5 4 3 2 1

Printed in the United States of America
ISBN 1-56955-319-X

Library of Congress Cataloging-in-Publication Data

Lutzer, Erwin W.
    Growing through conflict / Erwin Lutzer.
        p. cm.
    ISBN 1-56955-319-X (alk. paper)
    1. Conflict management in the Bible. 2. Conflict management—Religious aspects—Christianity. I. Title.
    BS680.C63 L87 2001
    248.8'6—dc21

                                                        2001002948

For Ben and Lisa Dykstra,
whose love for each other
and commitment to Christ
brings joy to our hearts.

Contents

Prologue

Some love it, others hate it, but all of us live with conflict. Some of our earliest recollections are of clashes with our brothers and sisters and disagreements with our parents. When we went to school we found ourselves in conflict with our classmates or our teachers. As adults we may find discord in our marriages, our workplace, or even in our church.

How we manage conflict tells us much about our personality and level of maturity. Some prefer to run and hide, steadfastly refusing to resolve disagreements. Wives often complain that their husbands ignore serious communication and prefer to "clam up or blow up."

Others—and all of us have met them—create conflict wherever they go. A peaceful room is turned into a battleground minutes after they enter. Minor issues are christened as major ones, and there is little room for disagreement. Such people have an ego need to create arguments and then win them at any cost.

David was thrust into conflict the moment he volunteered to fight Goliath. This was David's easiest battle, for he won it with one well-aimed stone. Never again was he to resolve a conflict that quickly. His conflict with Saul dragged on for ten years. His conflict with his wives made him the object of public ridicule. His conflict with his sons became a national scandal. He even had his conflicts with God.

The purpose of this book is to follow the life of David to benefit from his mistakes and failures, to learn how and how not to manage conflict. Often we think David was a cut above other servants of God, but we shall likely learn more from his weaknesses than from his strengths. Though David was mighty in battle, he was weak at home. Though he wrote poetry that soared to the heavens, he often was filled with depression and doubt. We will learn that God seldom removes us from conflict, but uses it to bring about spiritual maturity.

Join me on an adventure that will teach us how one sheep managed to stay with the Shepherd. We'll learn how God tempers the wind for the shorn lamb.

Despite David's failures—*glaring* failures—he was a "man after God's own heart." Though he died with his share of regrets, God Himself wrote his epitaph: "My servant David" (2 Sm 3:18).

That can be said about us, too, if we learn from this famous but flawed shepherd, turned king, who lived so long ago.

Chapter One

Conflict Within the Family
(Read 1 Samuel 16)

Did you know that it's impossible to predict who will be mightily used by God? Impossible, because God has His own reasons for putting unlikely people in even more unlikely places! His evaluation of each of us is quite different from the grade we give ourselves or the assessment of our friends. *It just may be that God has a place mapped out for you that is much greater than what you would ever dream for yourself.* Just ask David, the shepherd boy turned King of Israel!

We've all been measured by someone else's yardstick, evaluated by the personal preferences of our parents, siblings, and friends. In fact, we instinctively compare every person we meet with our standard of "most wanted qualities." Appearance, personality, wit, sincerity—all of these affect the judgments we make of one another. Though we might theoretically agree that all people are created equal, we grade one another on a scale that is according to our liking. We treat people not according to an absolute, but with relative value.

Parents make a mistake when they judge their children by society's yardsticks. Perhaps the most prevalent of those yardsticks is *beauty*, which James Dobson says our culture regards as the "gold coin of human worth." Parents often fall into the trap of paying more attention to the attractive child, the one who makes them feel best. The other children feel the pain of rejection, the depression that comes from knowing that they just do not measure up. Because our opinion of who we are is determined by those around us, the child who feels rejection by his parents will have emotional baggage to deal with as he or she struggles toward emotional wholeness.

If appearance is the *gold* coin of human worth, *intelligence* is surely the silver coin. If you have the good fortune of being a "whiz kid," you will be accepted because of your brilliance. There is prestige connected with high scores in algebra, political science, or computer programming.

Children may have natural abilities in music, art, or public speaking, and still feel the sting of rejection within the family network. Given the large number of dysfunctional families, even gifted children may grow up with feelings of depression and self-hatred. Children who are ignored or abused verbally or physically know the inner pain of feeling that no one really loves them, and that they have no apparent value.

There is evidence that David suffered because of rejection from his father and older brothers. They resented his quick ascendance to fame and would have preferred that he stay at home with the sheep where he belonged, but we're ahead of the story.

The Search for a King

As our story begins, King Saul had been rejected by God, and now the Lord said to Samuel, "How long will you grieve over

Saul, since I have rejected him from being king over Israel? Fill your horn with oil, and go; I will send you to Jesse the Bethlehemite, for I have selected a king for Myself among his sons" (1 Sm 16:1). So the aged Samuel made plans to go to Bethlehem to find a new king.

Already Saul was paranoid, filled with suspicion and hostility. Even the godly Prophet Samuel feared going to Bethlehem, lest the king discover the real reason for his mission. So the Lord graciously allowed Samuel, as a "pretext" for his trip, to offer a sacrifice when he arrived at Bethlehem (vv. 1-5). But after the crowd dispersed he privately fulfilled the real purpose for his journey. Jesse was proud when he was told that one of his sons would be the next king. In fact, he probably thought he knew in advance which of his sons it would be.

In the past, Samuel had often judged a person's character by his appearance—his posture, size, or personality. Thinking that this would be the natural way to determine which of the sons had been chosen by God, the seven young men strutted past Samuel one by one.

Quite naturally the eldest, Eliab, walked past first. Those who study the birth order charts tell us that firstborns are generally competitive, self-confident, and strong-willed. They usually make good leaders. Eliab probably carried a thick spear to demonstrate his bravery, and with his most kingly gait he walked past, confident that he would be chosen.

Even Samuel was fooled. "Surely the Lord's anointed is before Him," he thought to himself (v. 6). But as the old man became silent and listened to the voice of the Lord, he heard these astounding words: "Do not look at his appearance or at the height of his stature, because I have rejected him; for God *sees* not as man sees, for man looks at the outward appearance, but the Lord looks at the heart" (v. 7). The Almighty was talking. "I have rejected him!" What a blow to this proud, naturally gifted leader.

Then it was Abinadab who walked slowly past the prophet. By now Samuel had learned not to jump to conclusions, so he waited patiently for the divine voice. "Neither has the Lord chosen this one" (v. 8). Likewise all seven sons, fully dressed and armed, marched before Samuel, yet their kingly countenances did not impress the prophet. Each had to be told he had been rejected for kingship.

David, the Last Born

Samuel was puzzled. He assumed that all of Jesse's sons had been invited to this special party, but the line of sons came to an end and there was no divine confirmation. He couldn't help but wonder whether he had heard the voice of the Lord correctly. So he asked, "Are these all the children?" Jesse reluctantly answered, "There remains yet the youngest, and behold, he is tending the sheep." Then Samuel said, "Send and bring him; for we will not sit down until he comes here" (v. 11).

This is our first hint that David was not a favorite son. Jesse had been specifically invited to the sacrifice and told to bring his sons because one of them would be anointed king (vv. 1, 3). We get the impression that he had almost forgotten he had another son. His excuse for not having David present was weak, for there were others who could have been put in charge of the sheep (see 1 Sm 17:20). Perhaps he did not have high hopes for this boy.

This was probably not the first time David had been excluded from a family gathering; he had become accustomed to being relegated to tending sheep while his older brothers embarked on adventure.

Improbable as the request seemed, David was brought before the aging prophet. We can believe that David was pleasantly surprised that he was actually missed at the family gathering. When he was told that Samuel was there seeking to anoint a new king, he could scarcely believe it.

David was attractive, but not kingly. "Now he was ruddy, with beautiful eyes and a handsome appearance. And the Lord said, 'Arise, anoint him; for this is he'" (1 Sm 16:12). Samuel was just as certain that he was the right one as he was that the other sons were not! Samuel opened his flask and oil ran from David's head to his shoulders. And he was only fifteen years old!

Who was present at this anointing? We read, "Then Samuel took the horn of oil and anointed him in the midst of his brothers; and the Spirit of the Lord came mightily upon David from that day forward" (v. 13). David, the runt of the family, was anointed "in the midst of his brothers," as they were reeling from wounded pride, angry over what appeared to be God's arbitrary decision. The brother who was not even in the race had won the prize!

In most families, older brothers resent the younger ones, especially when they receive special honor. We do not even have to read between the lines to see that David was not loved by his brothers. The family simply could not bring itself to rejoice over the honor bestowed upon its youngest member.

We have glimpses of the derision the older brothers felt about their younger sibling. Though David had been anointed, he returned to herd the sheep and was treated as if nothing had happened. He soon learned that he was not enrolled in the school of royalty, but in the school of pain and disappointment. He continued his home responsibilities. Even when he was chosen to play the harp in the court of King Saul (vv. 18-23) he did not stop his work on the family farm, but went back and forth between the palace and his father's flock (1 Sm 17:15). Then the day arrived when his brothers' true feelings fully surfaced.

Let's skip ahead four years and catch a glimpse of how David's brothers felt about him. One day his father, Jesse, told David to take some food to his brothers. When he arrived he found that Goliath was challenging the armies of Israel. David began to ask questions about what was happening: "What will be done for the man who kills this Philistine, and takes away the reproach from Israel? For who is this uncircumcised Philistine, that he should taunt the armies of the living God?" (1 Sm 17:26).

David's oldest brother overheard the conversation, and we read, "Eliab's anger burned against David and he said, 'Why have you come down? And with whom have you left those few sheep in the wilderness? I know your insolence and the wickedness of your heart; for you have come down in order to see the battle'" (1 Sm 17:28).

Only last borns can fully appreciate the pain of such a tongue-lashing given by an older brother! If David was to be treated as a king-in-waiting, it would not be by his family! His anointing evidently meant little to them. His brothers treated him as if he didn't even deserve to know what was happening on the front lines. Parents and siblings are often the last to acknowledge greatness in their midst.

After Eliab scolded him, David replied, "What have I done now? Was it not just a question?" (1 Sm 17:29). Perhaps it was only a question, but younger brothers should know that they have no right to ask impertinent questions in the presence of older brothers.

With this exchange, Eliab passes from the pages of the Bible and is never heard from again. I have often thought about this confident firstborn who assumed that the selection process would be a beauty contest, dependent on who had the most impressive physique and most kingly presence. Yet he was passed over in silence, ignored, unrecognized for who he thought he was.

Though we are not told, I believe that Eliab's life was forever changed when he saw his kid brother anointed that afternoon in Bethlehem. Either he turned his heart to seek the Lord, content to play whatever part God gave him in Israel's history, or he died a resentful old man. Like Cain, who was angry with the favor shown to his younger brother, Abel, Eliab had the choice to turn to God for acceptance or to live with hatred and animosity.

David felt all of this rejection deeply, perhaps too deeply. Even in his later years he struggled with the indifference of his family toward him. As a grown man he would write, "For my father and my mother have forsaken me, but the Lord will take me up" (Ps 27:10). The conflict within his family was never far from his mind.

Perhaps on his way back to Ramah, Samuel speculated about why the other, more likely brothers were bypassed. If any one of them had become king, *he just might have been a clone of the vacillating Saul, who was impressive in appearance but had a self-serving, disobedient heart.* The text explicitly says that when Saul stood among the people, "he was taller than any of the people from his shoulders upward" (1 Sm 10:23). Yes, though Saul was tall and handsome, inwardly he was filled with rot. Looks are deceiving!

Long before Samuel actually anointed David in Bethlehem, God had said, "The Lord has sought out for Himself a man after His own heart, and the Lord has appointed him as ruler over His people" (13:14). In God's plan David had already been appointed king; it was just a matter of time before it would be fulfilled. A shepherd boy "after God's own heart" was chosen above those who appeared more qualified for the position.

Why did God reject seven rugged sons and call for the tagalong of the family? The answer is in 1 Samuel 16:7, a verse that deserves to be quoted a second time: "But the Lord said to Samuel, 'Do not look at his appearance or at the height of his stature, because I have rejected him; for God sees not as man sees, for man looks at the outward appearance, but the Lord looks at the heart.'"

God was making it clear that a man can be towering in stature and have a shriveled soul. A man can have all the qualifications for leadership, but if he lacks the qualities God values, he will be rejected by the One whose opinion counts the most.

An ancient prophet wrote, "For the eyes of the Lord move to and fro throughout the earth that He may strongly support those whose heart is completely His" (2 Chr 16:9). The Almighty is constantly taking inventory of us as individuals, and needless to say, He has access to information the rest of us lack. *When God measures a man He puts the tape around the heart and not the head.*

David, as we shall see, was far from perfect. In fact, he is often remembered for his glaring weaknesses. Yet he was used by God in spite of these faults, for God needed a broken-hearted man to teach future generations how to be comforted in the midst of pain. David was used by God, not in spite of these weaknesses, but *because of them!* How better could God display His grace than to show His power in the lives of those with the deepest inner needs? If we saw only David's strengths, we would not see God's grace.

What kind of heart did David have that he should attract the attention of the Almighty? Why David and not Eliab?

A Shepherd's Heart

Carefully read this divine commentary on why David was chosen: "He also chose David His servant, and took him from the sheepfolds; from the care of the ewes with suckling lambs He brought him, to shepherd Jacob His people, and Israel His inheritance. So he shepherded them according to the integrity of his heart, and guided them with his skillful hands" (Ps 78:70-72). David was simply promoted from one kind of shepherding to another! He took what he learned in the fields and applied it to leadership.

Out in the wild, David was willing to risk his life for one of the lambs. When explaining why he should be given the privilege of fighting Goliath, he said to Saul, "Your servant was tending his father's sheep. When a lion or a bear came and took a lamb from the flock, I went out after him and attacked him, and rescued *it* from his mouth; and when he rose up against me, I seized *him* by his beard and struck him and killed him" (1 Sm 17:34-35).

I certainly would not have taken on a lion or a bear simply to save some sheep. But given David's last-place status in the family, it was important that he accumulate a string of successes; he needed to carve out some territory that would give him recognition in the eyes of his family. So he became good at the responsibilities that came his way, even before he knew he would be given the high honor of kingship. Because of David's faithfulness with lambs, God would eventually make him the shepherd of the many lambs (His people) in Israel.

David served with selflessness and "the integrity of his heart." That means he could be trusted to be honest, dependable, and content with what he was given to do. He guided his flock skillfully; at night he returned with the same number of sheep as he had gone out with in the morning.

A thousand years later another shepherd would appear, born near where David had been anointed. Indeed, Bethlehem would then be known as the "City of David," the town where a virgin would spend the night and give birth to a son. He was the "Good Shepherd," who would eventually volunteer to "lay down His life for the sheep." God seems to be partial to shepherds!

Just look around and ask how many people are willing to take a risk for someone else, or to sacrifice for the good of others. How many of us are dependable, content to be faithful even when no one is looking? How many of us are willing to do the best we can with what we have?

If David could be trusted with sheep, God knew He could trust him with men. Faithfulness in the pasture was transferred to faithfulness in the palace.

A Humble Heart

When David was expected to return to tend sheep after being anointed, he did not insist that this was beneath his kingly dignity. Though he didn't have the New Testament, he understood its precept: "Humble yourselves, therefore, under the mighty hand of God, that He may exalt you at the proper time" (1 Pt 5:6). If we are faithful to where we are on the ladder, God will let us know when it is time for us to move up to the next rung.

David was willing to wait. Fortunately, he did not yet know that years of conflict with King Saul lay ahead of him. He would be hunted like a bird in the wilderness; he would have to duck to avoid spears and arrows. He would become so discouraged in his years of running that eventually he would defect to the enemy, joining the army of the Philistines!

For now all David needed to know was that if God had chosen him to be king, it would be up to God to fulfill His Word. God could be near him in the shadows just as much as in the light.

In all there would be fourteen years of waiting before David was crowned. Those years of emotional pressure were necessary for David to be drawn to God. He would learn that *what we do while we are waiting is just as important to God as that for which we wait!*

A Serving Heart

Two years after David was anointed, "The Spirit of the Lord departed from Saul, and an evil spirit from the Lord terrorized him" (1 Sm 16:14). David came into the king's court and used his skill as a musician to calm Saul's frenzy. This relieved Saul's depression; apparently the evil spirit receded in the presence of the hymns of praise played in honor of the Lord Jehovah. Even today, demonic spirits retreat in the presence of hymns of praise sung to the glory of God.

David also became Saul's armor bearer, showing that he was willing to play second fiddle. He was a king in waiting, but he knew that leadership involved being a servant. In fact, those who cannot serve cannot lead.

David didn't seek kingship. His brothers thought of many reasons they should have been chosen. They thought that kingship was a matter of self-confidence and ability. David knew that leadership in the kingdom was a choice that had to be left to God. *He never forgot whose kingdom it was.*

The best leaders, said Tozer, are those who do not aspire to leadership, but are conscripted by God. Those who wish to lead must learn to serve; they must wait for God to thrust them into the spotlight that leadership necessitates. Men choose leaders with one checklist, God uses another.

A Worshiping Heart

David, for all his faults, found satisfaction in his relationship with God. Little did he realize on that exciting afternoon in Bethlehem that he would experience years of pain—pain that would push him into the arms of God. "As the deer pants for the water brooks, so my soul pants for thee, O God. My soul thirsts for God, for the living God; when shall I come and appear before God?" (Ps 42:1-2). Read the Psalms and you will be convinced that David reached his greatest heights on the days when he had his greatest lows. He discovered, in the words of C.S. Lewis, that "God is the one all-satisfying object." Few people have learned to draw on God's resources as often and as desperately as David; few have found God to be so sufficient in the hour of need.

A Forgiven Heart

Many of us remember David for committing adultery with Bathsheba, and murdering Uriah in an attempt to cover up the sin. Although the consequences of those actions plagued David until the day he died, the other side of the coin is that he experienced the bliss of forgiveness (this story will be covered in detail in chapter 10). David came clean in his confession before the Lord. He was cleansed, forgiven, and restored. He offered God his broken heart, and the Lord put the pieces of his wounded soul back together.

The temptation is to judge a person by outward appearance. Those who don't meet our criteria are lost in the shuffle. God wants us to look beyond such superficial characteristics; He expects us to understand that the real person is what is within the heart. "For as he thinks within himself, so he is" (Prv 23:7).

Yes, sometimes it appears as if God puts His hand on the wrong man! He chooses those who would be considered least likely to succeed and elevates them to a position of responsibility.

Queen Victoria, it is said, told her friends that she thanked

God for the letter *m*. To explain, she would quote the words of Paul: "For consider your calling, brethren, that there were not many wise according to the flesh, not many mighty, not many noble; but God has chosen the foolish things of the world to shame the wise, and God has chosen the weak things of the world to shame the things which are strong, and the base things of the world and the despised, God has chosen, the things that are not, that He might nullify the things that are, that no man should boast before God" (1 Cor 1:26-29). Queen Victoria was thankful that Paul did not say, "Not *any* noble are chosen" but rather, "Not *many* noble are chosen." Little wonder she gave thanks for the letter *m!*

No, we cannot predict whom God will choose for positions of responsibility. He takes those who are in the shadows and brings them into the light. He takes someone whose family has "written him off," and inscribes his name in the Book of Life. The lowly are exalted and the mighty are brought low. "He raises the poor from the dust, and lifts the needy from the ash heap, to make *them* sit with princes, with the princes of His people" (Ps 113:7-8).

If you have felt neglected in your family; if you feel that God has forgotten about you while others are chosen for special privileges, take heart. Let God love you; let Him be the object of your concentration; do His will, whether great or small.

Take as much time as you need in His presence to point your heart like an arrow in His direction. Your friends have one opinion of you, God has another.

Guess whose matters most?

Chapter Two

Conflict With a Giant
(Read 1 Samuel 17)

There comes a time in every one of our lives when we are confronted by a threat that is twice our size. Whether it be cancer, bankruptcy, or a failed marriage—there is that unexpected menace that threatens to undo us.

Where do we turn?

Our character is often most clearly revealed by how we handle a crisis. Do we resort to manipulation, irrational anger, or even deceit? Or do we turn to God with the confidence that the Almighty is not overwhelmed by the crisis?

One of the most familiar stories in the Old Testament is the story of David and Goliath. It's a classic story of how a shepherd boy responded to a challenge that turned other men into cowards. It's also a story that teaches us how we can face our most painful giant without running for cover.

The historical context is familiar: Rather than have the armies of Israel and the Philistines fight a full-scale battle with extensive loss of life, there was an implied agreement that two representatives would duel, with the outcome determining which side won.

Think of the responsibility that rested on the shoulders of two men! How would you like your success or failure to determine the victory or slavery of your countrymen? The Philistines had no difficulty finding a volunteer:

> Then a champion came out from the armies of the Philistines named Goliath, from Gath, whose height was six cubits and a span. And he had a bronze helmet on his head, and he was clothed with scale-armor which weighed five thousand shekels of bronze. He also had bronze greaves on his legs and a bronze javelin slung between his shoulders. And the shaft of his spear was like a weaver's beam, and the head of his spear weighed six hundred shekels of iron; his shield-carrier also walked before him. And he stood and shouted to the ranks of Israel, and said to them, "Why do you come out to draw up in battle array? Am I not the Philistine and you servants of Saul? Choose a man for yourselves and let him come down to me.... I defy the ranks of Israel this day; give me a man that we may fight together."
>
> 1 SAMUEL 17:4-8, 10-11

To translate: Goliath was about nine feet tall with armor that weighed 125 pounds; his spear alone was 17 pounds. He was a classic picture of superhuman strength and defiance. As Alan Redpath describes him, "His head, his shoulders, his chest, and his legs were all clothed in brass—he was just a scintillating mass of brass, glittering in the Palestinian sun" (*The Making of a Man of God*, Fleming H. Revell, 1962, 21). For forty days he came forward, morning and evening, shouting his blasphemous defiance of Jehovah and challenging any Israelite to take him on.

Israel was having difficulty finding a volunteer! The nation's best troops were terrified, dismayed at the daily humiliation they were forced to endure. They were timidly pointing fingers at one another, each convinced that the other person should be the one to respond to the challenge.

Four years had passed since David had been privately anointed by Samuel in Bethlehem. Now, at age nineteen, he was still tending his father's flock, going back and forth between the sheep and Saul's court. He had no clear picture of how God intended to move him from shepherd to king. One day Jesse, his father, gave his youngest son an order to take some food to his brothers, who were at the scene of this nonbattle. His father also wanted a report on the progress of the fight, wondering whether anyone had had the nerve to challenge this blasphemer (vv. 17-19).

David went as quickly as he could, all the way to the battle line, where he joined his brothers, who were stationed on the hill at the head of the valley. At that moment Goliath appeared once more, cursing and taunting the men who faced him in the distance. Quickly, Israel's battle line moved ... *backward!* We read that all the men "fled and were greatly afraid" (v. 24).

David asked some questions: What has King Saul promised to the person who kills this Philistine? Who is this uncircumcised Philistine who thinks he can taunt the armies of the living God? Why can't this reproach be taken away from Israel? (v. 26)

As we already learned in the last chapter, Eliab, David's older brother, burned with anger at overhearing his youngest brother's conversation with the mighty men of Israel. "Little brother, go home!"

King Saul, however, heard a rumor that David might be his first volunteer. So he sent for this shepherd boy who begged for the opportunity to do battle with the despicable giant. Saul tried to talk David out of his heroism: "You are not able to go against this Philistine to fight with him; for you are but a youth while he has been a warrior from his youth" (v. 33).

David argued, however, that he and Goliath were much more evenly matched than the king realized. While tending sheep, David said, he had killed both a lion and a bear in the line of duty. More importantly, God would be on David's side in the skirmish. "The Lord who delivered me from the paw of the lion and from the paw of the bear, He will deliver me from the hand of this Philistine" (v. 37).

David was so convincing that Saul, whose hopes for any other prospect grew increasingly dim, decided he would give David a fighting chance. We know the rest of the story: David did what no other man in Israel thought possible. The giant's head was eventually presented to Saul on a platter!

Is there a situation in your life that is a reproach to the living God? Are you being harassed by Satan, whose taunts make you think your humiliation is assured? Are you up against a giant whose voice daily defies you? What giant blocks your path of spiritual progress?

Please remember that seldom are our giants wiped out as quickly as this one. I wish every spiritual battle could be won in a single day, with a single stone. David himself would eventually learn that this would be the only conflict God settled quickly for him. Most of his battles would drag on for years.

Yet, there are reasons why David became a "giant killer." The principles he used become a model for us as we face that big giant standing in the way of our spiritual progress. I believe there is more to this story than simply the remarkable fact that a boy killed a giant against such incredible odds. This is a picture of the spiritual conflict you and I participate in each day of our lives. It's the conflict between the true God and his blasphemous rivals.

When Goliath stood on the hill, he "cursed David by his gods" (v. 43). Who were these pagan deities? One would have been Dagon, the fish god with the head and hands of a man. Another would have been Baal-zebub, meaning, "Lord of flies." The flies apparently refer to dung beetles that crawled around on excrement and waste. These were the kinds of gods to which the Philistines sold their souls, but they were also the kind of gods Israel was supposed to hate, for behind them was the power of Satan himself.

David, as we shall see, came in the name of the living God. At stake in the eyes of these warring camps was the question: Whose God is the greatest? David was the only man who was willing to answer that question with more than words.

In a recent article, *National Geographic* noted that bull moose fight for dominance during the breeding season. They literally go head to head, with antlers crunching as they collide. Since their antlers are their only weapon, those who survive with theirs intact win. Broken antlers are a sure sign of defeat. Therefore, the battle fought in the fall is really won or lost during the summer, when the moose eat continually. The one that consumes the best diet for growing antlers and gaining weight will be the heavyweight in the fight. Those who eat inadequately sport weaker antlers and lose.

David won because he had developed some right habits

long before his battle with Goliath. Out on the hills of Bethlehem he spent many hours playing on his harp, developing his relationship with God. This special gift gave him an entrance to the highest court in the land. He was chosen to play for Saul simply because the king's servants sought the best harpist available. He also spent hours practicing with his sling; piles of rocks had been used in target practice. Trusting God for little things made it easier to believe when the life-threatening crisis came.

There were skillful soldiers in Israel, but David had something they did not possess. He understood the spiritual aspects of the conflict. Behind the very visible giant there were some powerful invisible forces. That's why this battle could be won only through faith in God.

What kind of faith kills giants?

Faith With Action

After David volunteered for this military assignment, Saul suggested that the boy wear the king's armor. So David tried on the bronze helmet, the long sword, and the heavy armor, but he concluded, "I cannot go with these, for I have not tested them" (1 Sm 17:39), and he took them off.

Saul wanted David to look as tough as Goliath. If they could meet on a level playing field, there might be an outside chance that David would win. Natural reason would suggest that we can only win a battle when we are as strong as, or stronger than, our enemy.

David, however, chose to meet the giant on different terms.

Yes, he was in good physical shape; yes, he had used a spear before; and yes, it made sense to wear thick armor. But that would not win against a man who had enormous physical strength and years of practice at throwing a spear. What is more, David correctly understood that this battle was primarily spiritual—*it was not just a conflict between two men, but between two gods.*

So David chose to meet this challenge with a method of fighting he had used before. He was more comfortable with a sling than with untested armor. He could believe God more easily with something he had successfully used than with cumbersome equipment that belonged to somebody else.

Here we see a beautiful blend between faith and works, faith and our best effort. Some people think that because the battle is the Lord's we should do nothing, but David knew that faith did not exclude fighting; *faith simply means that we fight with confidence.* David knew how accurately he could shoot and how close he would have to come to his target. He also knew that he could not win without God.

Skill alone could not win against this seasoned warrior. The stone might miss Goliath's temple and simply graze him. Or, the giant might duck as the stone whizzed over his head. David also knew that he would not have many chances, for the giant was skilled at throwing his spear. Perhaps this explains why David took only five stones: He knew there was no chance that he would get more than five opportunities to use his sling.

Let's not pour everyone into the same mold. Some are successful with a sling. Others can use a sword. But *no* human weapons can win in a spiritual battle. Whatever our gifts and talents, if they are not energized by God we will fail.

How often we fall into the trap of thinking that success comes by becoming like someone else. Dozens of books have been written on how so-and-so built a successful church, or how a man established a productive business. The implication is that when we follow the techniques of others we can duplicate their success.

David knew that whether he used Saul's armor or his own sling, ultimately, it was a matter of faith—faith that God would bless the means best for him. If it was really a battle between two gods, only the intervention of the true God could resolve the conflict.

No matter how excellent our strategy, God will let us fail if we put faith in the strategy rather than in Him. Regardless of our personal abilities, *spiritual forces can be fought only with spiritual weapons.* Satan cannot be fought with human resources, no matter how impressive they may be. Behind every human effort there must be faith in the power of the Almighty. Faith in God overcomes intimidations and the persistent voice of the enemy.

Unbelief said that Goliath was too big to hit; faith said he was too big to miss! Yet David knew that faith was not static; faith meant that he would have to be personally involved in a venture which, humanly speaking, involved great personal risk.

Faith With Authority

Goliath couldn't believe his eyes! In the distance he saw a boy come toward him who wasn't even dressed in armor! We read, "When the Philistine looked and saw David, he disdained him;

for he was *but* a youth, and ruddy, with a handsome appearance" (1 Sm 17:42). Surely this was some kind of joke!

The giant rehearsed his stock speech, but it was given with even more contempt. "Am I a dog, that you come to me with sticks?... Come to me, and I will give your flesh to the birds of the sky and the beasts of the field" (vv. 43-44).

David replied, "You come to me with a sword, a spear, and a javelin, but I come to you in the name of the Lord of hosts, the God of the armies of Israel, whom you have taunted. This day the Lord will deliver you up into my hands, and I will strike you down and remove your head from you ... that all the earth may know that there is a God in Israel" (vv. 45-46).

What did it mean for David to come to Goliath "in the name of the Lord ... of the armies"? There are many different names for God in the Bible, simply because there are so many different aspects to His character. An effective prayer is one that appeals to the attribute of God that corresponds to the present obstacle.

When we need provision, God becomes to us, "Jehovah-Jireh" (Gn 22:14); when we need peace He is "Jehovah-Shalom" (Jgs 6:24); when we need a banner to lead us He is "Jehovah-Nissi" (Ex 17:15). And when we are in combat we rely upon "Jehovah-Sabaoth," used here by David as "the Lord of Armies."

David affirmed that Jehovah is, after all, the "commander-in-chief" of the invisible angels, the armies of heaven. He appealed to God's military title to win this military victory.

How could David presume to say, "I come in the name of the Lord"? Wherein was David's authority? First, he knew that he was a representative of God. He was coming on behalf of the honor of another. The rebel on earth would be fought by the forces of heaven. Second, David knew that the giant himself did not have any rights. *Goliath was standing on territory that God had given to the tribe of Judah.* The land the Philistine sought to defend was, in effect, stolen. The very ground he used to launch his insults had been deeded to those whom he foolishly sought to defy!

The tragedy, of course, is that Goliath's bluff was working. The Israelites to whom the land had been given stood in fear, not knowing how to end the forty days of humiliation. They simply did not know how to translate the promises of God into a military victory.

Then David came along in the name of the "God of armies." The giant relied on his god; David relied on His; and the outcome proved which deity was the most powerful.

Faith With the Right Motive

Why did David crave victory? Was it to make his name great? Was it to solve a problem or make life easier? No, it was to take away the reproach of a nation that belonged to God. The embarrassment they endured was a disgrace that made the Almighty Himself appear inept, unable to rise to the catcalls of this pagan.

Every time the men of Israel ran from this giant the name of God was being dragged in the mud. Children were growing up in Israel without any clear models that vindicated God's believability. The entire nation bore an unshakeable loser's stigma. As David put it, this scandal was causing "the enemies of the Lord to blaspheme."

David predicted that this pagan's head would soon be cut off and the armies of the Philistines would become food for the birds, "that all the earth may know that there is a God in Israel, and that all this assembly may know that the Lord does not deliver by sword or by spear; for the battle is the Lord's and he will give you into our hands" (1 Sm 17:46-47).

Then David ran toward the Philistine, whirling the sling faster and faster over his head and then releasing one of the two strings. "And David put his hand into his bag and took from it a stone and slung it, and struck the Philistine on his forehead. And the stone sank into his forehead, so that he fell on his face to the ground" (v. 49). God himself guided the minute movements of David's arm and directed the stone at the one unprotected, vital spot—Goliath's forehead.

And so it was that God used an improbable shepherd boy with a dubious weapon to strike the Philistine. The first stone flung in faith by David's arm did what the combined armies of Israel could not do.

God only knows how many battles we have lost because our motives have been selfish. We have called on the name of the Lord to bolster our reputations, to make life easier, or to prove we were right. Only the pure motive of defending the honor of God is effective as we wrest God's territory from God's enemy.

Faith With Humility

With Goliath lying on the ground, breathing his last, David ran up to finish the job. He pulled the giant's own spear out of its sheath to cut off his head.

This was a high moment, a moment to gloat, to remind his family that they had misjudged their last born, but that is not what David did. Yielding to God is difficult before a battle; it is almost impossible after a victory! The temptation to take at least a bit of the credit is powerful.

Both armies were watching breathlessly to see which champion would be alive after the duel. When David was seen standing over his fallen foe, the startled Philistines fled. As for King Saul and his men, we read, "And the men of Israel and Judah arose and shouted and pursued the Philistines as far as the valley, and to the gates of Ekron. And the slain Philistines lay along the way to Shaaraim, even to Gath and Ekron. And the sons of Israel returned from chasing the Philistines and plundered their camps" (vv. 52-53).

Finally the men of Israel entered the battle! Now that the Philistines were fleeing, they had the courage to chase them! Probably years later they told their grandchildren about their bravery in fighting the enemies of God. Yes, it is true that *success has many fathers, but failure is an orphan.*

The name of God was vindicated in Israel. That evening as the mothers tucked their children into bed, they could give conclusive proof that Jehovah was mightier than the gods of the Philistines. The stigma of defeat lifted like a dark cloud from Israel.

Concluding Lessons

First, no giant is bigger than God. This is not to say that our battles will be won as easily as taking a stone from a sling and whipping it in the direction of the enemy. As we mentioned, David himself will find out that God does not always take problems away that quickly.

But our giants must always be compared to God, not to ourselves. Size is a matter of relationship; it is a matter of perspective.

Second, *our giants are as big as we believe them to be.* If we think they are formidable, they are. As long as Israel believed that Goliath could not be beaten, he couldn't be!

In our day, believers are becoming much better educated regarding spiritual warfare. The reality of Satan in our society can no longer be denied, and Christians are fighting him through prayer and submission to God. But along with this new awareness, there is a danger that we might begin to think Satan is stronger than he actually is; we might so emphasize his power that we eclipse the power of God.

Third, *we cannot fight Goliath if we have even partial allegiance to pagan gods.* To the extent that we are not under the authority of Christ we will be unable to exercise our authority as believers. God does not deliver us if we refuse to repent of our double-mindedness.

Sometimes the Goliath in my heart is a greater threat than the giant on my path. God may want us to live with some giants; He may not remove our irritations, our domestic or vocational conflicts. He uses our battles to purify our hearts, to bring to light those sins that we have so confidently hidden.

Those giants that keep us from our freedom in Christ—addictions, fears, or bitterness—are giants that God wants us to conquer in His name. Faith does not mean that we always kill the giant; sometimes it means only that the giant no longer plagues us. The freedom of the heart should be our goal.

When fighting our giants we must always return to the basics. There are no secret weapons, just faith nurtured by absorbing the Word of God into our lives. Tackling a giant means that we are willing to submit to all that God has already taught us. Like David, we must remember that the lessons we learn when confronted with smaller battles will prepare us for the bigger ones.

The God in whose name David fought Goliath is the One who is on our side in our spiritual conflicts. With the right kind of faith, we, too, can participate in winning a victory.

This was the easiest battle David ever fought. From now on, he would feel the pain of long, protracted conflict.

Chapter Three

Conflict Among Kings
(Read 1 Samuel 18-19)

Have you ever had to wait for the results of an operation? Or wait for several years to find the job you have always wanted? Minutes can seem like hours and hours like days. Patience, someone has said, is learning to idle your engine when you would like to strip your gears. God often goes to great lengths to teach His servants how to wait.

The sun was beginning to set on King Saul's reign, and it was beginning to rise on David's. Saul had been told that God had rejected him and another had been found to take his place (see 1 Sm 13:14). Later, David would be anointed in Bethlehem without Saul's knowledge. The stage was set for the transfer of power. But the Almighty appeared in no hurry to fulfill His Word.

For ten long years Saul pursued David and tried to kill him. David experienced the full range of human emotion, vacillating between hope and despair. Sometimes he was encouraged by God's special protection; at other times he resorted to desperation, even joining the Philistine army. Yet God was working to perfect David even while at the same time he was judging King Saul.

There is a third man who becomes part of this story, and his name is Jonathan. Jonathan was next in line to be king, to succeed his father in the monarchy, but when he learned that David had been anointed, he willingly submitted to the will of God. He made a covenant with David: "And Jonathan stripped himself of the robe that was on him and gave it to David, with his armor, including his sword and his bow and his belt" (18:4). He gladly gave the symbols of kingship to his trusted friend.

This son was as different from his father as light is from darkness. If anyone should ever doubt that children do not have to follow in the flawed footsteps of their fathers, just think of Jonathan. He gladly relinquished his right to kingship. In contrast, his father was willing to resort to murder to keep his fragile hold on the throne.

David was caught in the middle, between Jonathan's love and Saul's hate. He had to learn to wait and let God work out the obstacles that stood in the way of his becoming king.

These two kings stand in sharp contrast in the way they responded to the circumstances of life. They illustrate the two different attitudes we can have when thrown into a situation that strikes at the heart of our pride, our opportunities, and our rights. They portray two different attitudes toward *ruling* in God's kingdom.

Jealousy Versus Humility

Saul had a promising beginning. The people wanted a king, and the Prophet Samuel was told by the Lord that he would find a man who would be anointed to rule the people of Israel and deliver the nation from the hand of the Philistines. "When Samuel saw Saul, the Lord said to him, 'Behold, the man of whom I spoke to you! This one shall rule over My people'" (1 Sm 9:17). Then Samuel anointed him in obedience to the word of the Lord.

The Holy Spirit had touched Saul's heart: "When they came to the hill there, behold, a group of prophets met him; and the Spirit of God came upon him mightily, so that he prophesied among them" (10:10). On the day of his public coronation, Saul had appeared to be so humble that he hid himself from the people (v. 22).

Saul had everything Christians seek today. He was empowered by the Spirit, had the gift of prophecy, and at times exerted powerful leadership. He was naturally gifted, rallied the people to his cause, and defeated the Ammonites and Philistines. The people had every reason to believe that he was the very leader the nation needed. Yes, he was the Lord's anointed.

Saul, however, had one fatal flaw: *He saw the kingdom as belonging to himself and not God.*

This error of perception caused him to fear the people more than he feared God. He was more concerned about his reputation than about obedience. His vacillating temperament kept those around him off balance. One day he appeared to be compassionate, and the next day he was a raving maniac. Through these unpredictable moods, he kept those around him in fearful bondage and control.

Eventually, Saul became self-deceived. Many times he promised that he would change; the future would be different from the past (19:6). He admitted that he had sinned and even confessed to having played the fool (26:21). But he always returned to his paranoia, and eventually sought the counsel of a witch (28:7-25).

This explains why Saul chafed against the Almighty's word that the kingdom would be taken from him. Though God's decision was not arbitrary, but based on a clear case of disobedience, Saul would not accept his fate. He simply refused to see it God's way. God had no right to take the kingdom from him.

Saul felt threatened, determined to keep his job. He looked around, wondering whom God had chosen to succeed him, and his evil eye fell upon David, the talented young man whose fame had spread throughout the land. Saul became obsessed with jealousy and fear.

Initially, Saul loved David even when the young man had stolen the limelight by defeating Goliath. He even set David over his men of war and noticed that he prospered. Yet there were moments when Saul could not forget the cheers of the women when David returned from killing Goliath: "Saul has slain his thousands, And David his ten thousands," they sang, accompanied by musical instruments (18:7). And the whole nation was watching!

Jealousy burned within Saul's heart. "They have ascribed to David ten thousands, but to me they have ascribed thousands. Now what more can he have but the kingdom?" (v. 8). From then on Saul looked on David with deep suspicion and anger. David, the young man whom Saul had appointed as leader over the army, this man who owed his entire career to Saul's influence and prestige, was in line to inherit the kingdom! Saul's envy was inflamed with murderous rage.

David, by contrast, did not seem to be obsessed with his own popularity. Though he was practically worshiped by the masses for his bravery and military prowess, he was aware that God would have the final say in his life. He did not seek the place of leadership, but willingly entrusted his fate to God who gives the kingdoms of this world to whomever He wills.

Waiting for God becomes difficult when we see other people succeed at the very point where we are failing. One of the most painful assignments is to live in the shadow of someone who is a greater success; someone whose visible achievements dwarf our own meager efforts.

Envy is found everywhere. A missionary worker told me, "Nothing would delight my coworkers more than if I were to fail!" There is a little bit of Saul in every human heart. And where there is envy, there is every evil work.

Gene Edward wrote: "Saul is in your bloodstream, in the marrow of your bones. He makes up the very flesh and muscle of your heart. He is mixed into your soul. He inhabits the nuclei of your atoms. King Saul is one with you" (*A Tale of Three Kings*, Christian Books, 1980, pp. 21-22).

If we don't confess and forsake the sin of envy, we will find it difficult to trust God; for Christ asked, "How can you believe, when you receive glory from one another, and you do not seek the glory that is from the *one and* only God?" (Jn 5:44). We aren't submissive until we can give thanks to God for those who are more successful than we are.

Unfortunately, Saul was never able to conquer the beast that rose up within him. He simply could not commit the kingdom to God; it had to be his and his alone. F.B. Meyer wrote, "Happy had Saul been if he had trodden the hell-born spark of jealousy beneath his feet, or extinguished it in a sea of prayer" (*David: Shepherd, Psalmist, King,* Zondervan, 1953, 49).

The humble man is willing to step aside when someone else comes along with more ability; the proud man will not budge though dwarfed by those around him. The humble man knows the kingdom is God's; the other holds it to his heart at any cost.

Saul simply would not recognize God's authority as owner of the kingdom. He would not resign even though the Almighty had spoken. He acknowledged his own kingship and none other.

Manipulation Versus Trust

Saul hoped to manipulate the outcome of events. Though God had spoken, he evidently thought he could overturn God's plans. If he killed David, his grasp on the crown would be secure.

Saul had been plagued with bouts of melancholy and depression, and David, you will recall, had been recruited to play the harp in his court. One day, Saul began to rave while David was playing. He grabbed a spear, "And Saul hurled the spear for he thought, 'I will pin David to the wall.' But David escaped from his presence twice" (1 Sm 18:11).

Embarrassed at having failed, Saul tried to set David up so that the Philistines would kill him. Specifically, he promised David his older daughter, Merab, as a wife and then planned to appoint him to fight the Philistines. The intention was that David would engage the Philistines, who would (Saul hoped) kill him in battle. But the plan backfired, for David would not accept the king's generous proposal. Merab became the wife of another man, and David did not do battle with the Philistines.

Saul had another plan. Another one of his daughters, Michal, loved David. Saul encouraged the wedding for one good reason: He hoped that Michal would become a snare to David. Saul assumed that once David married Michal, the Philistines would make David a target and kill him. He told his servants to tell David that he loved him and would like to have him as a son-in-law.

Saul then stipulated one small price for marrying his daughter: one hundred foreskins of the Philistines! Saul hoped that David would be killed while trying to meet this quota, but David and his men killed twice as many Philistines as requested, and so paid his dowry without any harm coming to them (v. 27).

Saul was stunned by David's successes. We read, "When Saul saw and knew that the Lord was with David, and *that* Michal, Saul's daughter, loved him, then Saul was even more afraid of David. Thus Saul was David's enemy continually" (vv. 28-29). To Saul's horror, David's popularity continued to rise.

All of this should have been a signal to remind Saul that he should repent and give up his attempts to kill David. Why not simply accept God's verdict? This was the opportunity for him to come to his senses. But his heart was hardened.

Something else should have touched Saul's calloused heart—the tender humility of his son Jonathan. Saul knew right well that his son loved David, and yet the paranoid king had the gall to ask Jonathan to put David to death (19:1).

Saul's irrational rage only bonded Jonathan and David

more closely together. Rather than putting David to death, Jonathan helped him escape. Jonathan asked David to hide, so that he could ask his father what his true intentions were. In a touching scene, Jonathan pleaded with his father not to sin against David, who had done no harm. He urged his father to accept David rather than destroy him (vv. 4-6).

Saul listened to his son Jonathan and agreed that David should not be put to death. So David returned to Saul's court in the vain hope that the feud was over, but it was not to be. Once again an evil spirit terrorized Saul, and he tried to kill David while he was playing the harp. David fled, just as the spear struck the wall behind him. This time his wife, Michal, let David out of the house in a basket, to spare him from her deranged father (vv. 10-12).

Despite his schizophrenia, there were times when Saul still exercised his spiritual gift of prophecy. "The Spirit of God came upon him also, so that he went along prophesying continually until he came to Naioth in Ramah" (v. 23). This mixture of carnality and giftedness; this paranoia and spiritual perception exists in all leaders who will not acknowledge God as the owner of their kingdom.

Contrast this with David. Sometime later David was hiding from Saul in the wilderness of Engedi, and Saul took three thousand men and went to look for him. Incredibly, Saul came into the very cave where David was hiding. David was so near to Saul that he secretly cut off the edge of Saul's robe. Yet afterward, when David's men wondered why he hadn't killed his enemy, David said it bothered his conscience that he had even cut off a bit of Saul's coat: "Far be it from me because of the Lord that I should do this thing to my lord, the Lord's anointed, to stretch out my hand against him, since he is the Lord's anointed" (24:6). He instructed his men not to kill Saul.

Later, David spared Saul's life a second time when Saul and his men were sleeping on a plateau in the wilderness (the details will be discussed later). Why didn't David use these opportunities to kill this enemy who was trying to kill *him*? Why would David not put forth his hand to touch the Lord's anointed?

David understood that the kingdom belonged to God, and that no man should be elevated to leadership unless God brought it about. If Saul is to fall, let God bring him down! For as long as he was able, David was a loyal subject of Saul's kingdom. Under no conditions would he take it upon himself to oust the leader God had installed. God alone raises up; God alone brings down.

We all have our Goliaths, but we also live with our Saul who never seems to go away. Some wives have husbands who have made life miserable; employees have employers who have done all they could to make earning a living as painful as possible. Pray as we might that these situations be changed, they simply will not go away quickly. We are convinced that it would not upset some eternal plan if God were to remove our obstacles, yet He lets them drag on until His purpose is accomplished.

There are some things we can control, but others are out of our hands. Manipulation, in whatever form, is proof that we do not really trust God. The man who told me that he has to cheat on an application form in order to get a job is taking his life out of the hands of God and putting it in his own control. Is not God able to lead us without the need to resort to dishonesty? When we trust God against incredible odds, it just may turn out to be His finest moment in our lives. "Lord, let me change what I can; be submissive in those things that I cannot; and have the grace to tell the difference," someone prayed.

Manipulation has many faces, among which are *dishonesty* and *guilt*. "If you don't marry me, I will commit suicide!" We've all heard such remarks coming from people who rebel against leaving their future wholly with God. I know a family smothered by the gifts and favors of a manipulative woman, who expects this family will limit their friendships to her alone. She becomes resentful of others who intrude on this "close relationship."

Bribery, gossip, planning pitfalls—these are just a few of the different ways manipulation rears its ugly head. It is an unmistakable sign of one who simply will not trust God with the details of his or her life. It's also a sign of someone who, like Saul, may be rife with spiritual gifts and natural talent, but is willing to throw spears when his or her ego is threatened.

Understand that Saul could easily rationalize his actions. Was he not the anointed of the Lord? Did he not have the gift of prophecy? Could he not point to a string of military victories? There are discredited Christian leaders today who have built similar shields of rationalization that keep them insulated from the facts. Long after their scheming has disgraced them; long after they have destroyed others by their selfishness and greed, they still pretend that their lives are beyond reproach. Like Saul, their lives become a grand charade.

Many times our prayers are nothing more than expressions of worry and manipulative anxiety. Prayer in itself is not as powerful as honest submission, the committing of a conflict to God, awaiting His resolution of the outcome. The test of true commitment is whether we can rest in the knowledge that the outcome has been transferred from our shoulders to God's.

For David, Goliath was one problem; Saul was quite another. There was no dramatic answer to the threat of this paranoid madman. God just let the problem drag on, year after year, until David thought that the Almighty had long forgotten about His promise. Why? God was teaching David to wait. He had enrolled him in the school of brokenness.

Gene Edward suggests that if David had not experienced ten years of pain, he would have grown up to be "King Saul II," but God used the external King Saul to "cut away the Saul inside David's heart. The operation, by the way, took years and was a brutalizing experience that almost killed the patient," (*A Tale of Three Kings*, Christian Books, 22).

The impatience of Saul did little to slow his eventual demise. It revealed a heart that was in direct opposition to the will and purpose of God. *It revealed a heart that would not let God be God in His own kingdom. A heart that was obsessed with its own importance.*

The Holy Spirit and an Evil Spirit

Behind the conflict between David and Saul was a battle between God and Satan. Many Christians are surprised to read, "Now it came about on the next day that an evil spirit from God came mightily upon Saul" (1 Sm 18:10). Why would an evil spirit from the Lord come upon Saul? Remember that evil spirits are ultimately under God's direction and control. All of their work, yes, even the most evil, is done under God's meticulous supervision. So if He wants an evil spirit to come upon an individual, He simply withdraws His protective hand and the spirit begins the harassment.

This was a judgment, a form of discipline, to bring out the worst or the best in a man who had already hardened his heart against the Lord. Like Pharaoh, whose heart was hardened, so Saul's jealousy was magnified through the direct agency of Satan.

The result? Saul became a paranoid-schizophrenic, filled with murderous envy. His heart turned from dark to darker and darkest, inflamed with the passion of murder and revenge. Here, for all the world to see, was a man devoid of self-control, given over to the compulsions of an evil spirit.

Please notice the irony: It was Saul who removed all the witches from the land (28:3); yet when pushed into a corner, he himself went to a witch, the very person his subjects were forbidden to see! Like many others who preach one thing and do another, Saul considered himself the one grand exception to his own rules!

Why does God anoint men who are unworthy of power? Gene Edward writes, "He says 'yes' to some very unworthy vessels.

"He gives unworthy men power? His power? Even though they are a pile of dead men's bones inside?

"Why does God do such a thing? The answer is both simple and shocking. He sometimes gives unworthy vessels a greater portion of power so that it might eventually be revealed for all to see the *true* state of internal nakedness within that man" (p. 40). *God is still in the business of revealing human hearts for what they are.*

Why do some people who repent remain unchanged? Why does a husband who promises his wife that he will never again commit adultery do it again? Why does an alcoholic swear off alcoholism only to be ensnared again? Why did Saul's sincere attempts at repentance accomplish nothing?

The answer is that Saul repented only halfheartedly. There was always a catch; some condition always accompanied his tears. Early on he said to Samuel the prophet, "I have sinned; but please honor me now before the elders of my people" (15:30). Notice: "I have sinned ... but honor me!"

If Saul had repented with a whole heart, he would have resigned from the kingship and turned it over to David, whom he knew had been chosen by God for the crown. But Saul could never bring himself to such submission; *even his repentance was a form of manipulation—an effort to have it his way.*

I've counseled wives who have lived with husbands who have Saul's characteristics: prone to violence, repeated broken promises, and personality changes. They will even use a repentant attitude to gain sympathy, but all the while they are still hiding from the full truth. Thus, like Saul, Satan works to defeat and destroy their intention to change.

I've known Christian leaders who have Saul's characteristics: insecure, fearful of the success of others, willing to destroy potential threats, and totally committed to protecting their turf. They may also be anointed teachers, gifted organizers, and good spear throwers!

The only answer is the one that Saul did not accept: total repentance. He should have realized that God had a right to give the kingdom to whomever He wished.

Lessons About Repentance

From Saul we can learn some priceless lessons about repentance. First, *if we repent with only half a heart, God will no longer come to our aid.* Such people, says James, should not expect to have their prayers answered, but are like the surf of the sea, driven and tossed by the wind—"being a double-minded man, unstable in all his ways" (Jas 1:8). Halfhearted repentance brings us under the discipline of God.

When Saul became desperate, he did not turn to God but to Satan, to the witch at Endor. Incredibly, he told the woman he wanted to speak to Samuel, the very man whose counsel he had consistently ignored. I believe God did a miracle and actually brought Samuel out of his grave. Only such a miracle explains the terror of the medium (1 Sm 28:12).

In speaking to Samuel, Saul said some of the saddest words ever uttered by a human being: "God has departed from me and answers me no more, either through prophets or by dreams; therefore I have called you, that you may make known to me what I should do" (v. 15). Samuel chided Saul for coming to him and explained that the kingdom would be taken from him, saying, "God has become your adversary."

Either God will have our whole heart or Satan will seek to get it all. Any middle ground is difficult to maintain.

Second, *repentance involves unconditional surrender, the acknowledgment that God, not man, is in charge.* The anointed in Christendom who lead with a great display of gifts but who also squash their rivals through manipulation, innuendo, and skewed criticism—such must be brought to total surrender no matter the cost. Only then will they stop hurling spears, quit manipulating events, and cease fighting those who are really on their team. But the Saul in our hearts is loath to die.

Those who have the spirit of Saul expect the submission of all those in their kingdom, but they themselves will not submit to God. The kingdom is theirs, not the Lord's.

What distinguished David from Saul was his understanding of submission. When Saul faced death, he went to a medium; when David faced death, he went to God.

In God's presence David discovered the power of the Holy Spirit, who had come upon him when he was anointed in Bethlehem (16:13). David felt the full force of Saul's death threats, but he left Saul's future to God. In a psalm written during his troubles with Saul, he prayed:

> Deliver me from my enemies, O my God; set me securely on high away from those ... who do iniquity, and save me from men of bloodshed. For behold, they have set an ambush for my life; fierce men launch an attack against me, not for my transgression nor my sin, O Lord, for no guilt of mine, they run and set themselves against me. Arouse Thyself to help me, and see!
>
> PSALM 59:1-4

Yet David did not end his prayer in anguish, for he knew that God would ultimately protect and vindicate him. As has been said so often, "Men are immortal till their work is done." The psalm ends:

> But as for me, I shall sing of Thy strength; yes, I shall joy-fully sing of Thy loving-kindness in the morning, for

Thou hast been my stronghold, and a refuge in the day of my distress. O my strength, I will sing praises to Thee; for God is my stronghold, the God who shows me loving-kindness.

PSALM 59:16-17

Saul grasped for the kingdom but eventually God caused it to slip away from him. David refused to grasp it and it was given to him in God's time. Saul was impatient with God and was abased; David waited for God and was exalted.

When we wait for God, we don't lose time; and when we run ahead of God we don't gain time.

"Rest in the Lord, and wait patiently for Him: fret not thyself because of him who prospereth in his way, because of the man who bringeth wicked devices to pass" (37:7, KJV).

"Wait on the Lord, and keep His way, and He shall exalt thee to inherit the land: when the wicked are cut off, thou shalt see it" (v. 34).

Those who believe the kingdom belongs to God can wait to be exalted. Those who believe that the kingdom belongs to themselves throw spears at potential rivals.

They also experience the discipline of God.

Chapter Four

Conflict With Doubt
(Read 1 Samuel 20-23)

Success in our spiritual battles is usually an uphill fight; but we can coast to defeat without so much as a whimper. How quickly and effortlessly we can slide into a series of small decisions that land us in a tangled web from which there is no easy exit.

A Christian man who began to make small bets on sporting events with his peers in the office soon graduated to larger and more promising gambling ventures. Within three years he found himself in a racket that had ties to the underworld. When he was indicted and convicted of a series of crimes, his family and friends were shocked. So was he. He couldn't believe that what began as a bit of fun with petty cash had suddenly mushroomed into a life of deception, greed, and cruelty.

A young Christian woman caught up in a moment of passion became sexually involved with her boyfriend. Though they were intimate only once, she became pregnant. Because of her excellent reputation everyone was surprised, incredulous that this could happen to such nice young people. She dropped out of college, kept the baby, and in bitterness turned against her family and her church. After this she became intimate with a number of different men, and even today is still groping, unable to find her way in life. The power of one wrong decision!

David, the man after God's own heart, buckled under the pressure of years of being hounded by King Saul. He was weary of living like a fugitive, like a mouse chased by a hawk. Eventually, he was not only running from Saul but also, unwittingly, running from God. When he thought he couldn't take it anymore, he made a series of wrong decisions, lost his spiritual orientation, and lived as if the God he had come to know no longer cared.

Saul was relentless in his determination to put David to death. David, as we have learned, had escaped from his own house and was now forced to be on the run, keeping a few steps ahead of the demented king. Although Jonathan initially thought that his father's hostility was past, subsequent events proved otherwise. When David failed to show up at a feast, Saul interpreted this to mean that he was plotting mischief. (The king may also have been angry because he was planning to kill David at this banquet!)

Saul was filled with anger when he saw David's empty chair. "Then Saul's anger burned against Jonathan and he said to him, 'You son of a perverse, rebellious woman! Do I not know that you are choosing the son of Jesse to your own shame and to the shame of your mother's nakedness? For as long as the son of Jesse lives on the earth, neither you nor your kingdom will be established. Therefore now, send and bring him to me, for he must surely die'" (1 Sm 20:30-31).

When Jonathan protested on David's behalf, Saul, in a fit of rage, did the unthinkable: He hurled his spear at Jonathan, intending to kill him! The angry king tried to kill his own son, whose only crime was to love David! Though we are surprised by how debased this demented king became, perhaps we should not be: *When our kingdom becomes our god, we will even sacrifice our children to protect it.*

Jonathan was now convinced that there was no possibility of reconciliation between his father and his friend. He realized that David had been quite right in saying, "As your soul lives, there is hardly a step between me and death" (v. 3). David hid in a cave, and Jonathan, using the signal of two arrows, let him know that he must become a fugitive, hiding out wherever he could.

What follows is a scene too sensitive to reconstruct. David and Jonathan met, knowing it could be the last time, saying their good-byes, promising only that they would love each other till death. They kissed and wept, but David wept much more. Finally, Jonathan said to David, "Go in safety, inasmuch as we have sworn to each other in the name of the Lord, saying, 'The Lord will be between me and you, and between my descendants and your descendants forever.' Then he rose and departed, while Jonathan went into the city" (v. 42).

When David fled, he could have taken part of the army with him. If he had done that, he might have been just another King Saul, insisting on having his own turf, but David knew that the kingdom was not his. He would not lift a finger to hasten his own kingship or to shorten the reign of Saul.

David was about twenty years old when he was driven into the wilderness to spare his life. When we remember that he was thirty years old when he was finally crowned king in Hebron (2 Sm 5:4), we know that he was beginning the life of a fugitive, a harried existence that would last for ten long years.

I believe that David had some insecurities that made him

greatly desire the favor of King Saul. But he had failed in that, and now he also had to say good-bye to Jonathan, which almost brought him to the breaking point.

That was when David began a series of decisions that brought him embarrassment, shame, and eventually grief. This was not a high point in his distinguished career.

Here are two snapshots of David.

David in Panic

Often we say rather glibly, "Trust in God and all will be well." But sometimes we trust and it isn't well at all. David's trust in God did not rid him of Saul's hatred; it did not allow him to remain united with his family. Though he trusted, he had to flee to spare his life.

Running in panic he came to Nob, just north of Jerusalem, where the tabernacle of Israel had been erected. The priest, Ahimelech, was disturbed to see David. He knew that there was a price on David's head, so he was reluctant to get involved.

"Why are you alone and no one with you?" he asked.

David replied, "The king has commissioned me with a matter, and has said to me, 'Let no one know anything about the matter on which I am sending you and with which I have commissioned you; and I have directed the young men to a certain place.' Now therefore, what do you have on hand? Give me five loaves of bread, or whatever can be found" (1 Sm 21:1-2).

With that, David took a step on the slippery slope of dishonesty that eventually cost him his reputation and dignity.

Obviously, Saul had not sent him on a secret mission, and there may not have been any young men with him as he claimed.

David told this lie to alleviate any suspicions that the priest might have, and to get something to eat. Although there was no ordinary bread available, there was some shewbread which had been consecrated, bread which should be eaten only by priests or those who were ceremonially pure (see Lv 24:9). Centuries later, Christ cited this story with approval, pointing out that life is more holy than bread (Mt 12:3-4, 7-8). Christ was not giving His approval to David's decision to go to Nob; He simply was saying that human need is of greater importance than a ritual.

The problem was not the bread that David ate but the lie that he told. Although he thought it would help him in his flight from Saul, the truth eventually surfaced and he was in an even worse predicament. Doeg, a friend of Saul who happened to be in the tabernacle at the time, later told Saul what he had seen and heard (1 Sm 22:9).

In the end, David's dishonesty only opened him up to greater deceptions. First, he *told* a lie, then he *believed* one. He asked the priest to lend him a sword or a spear that he could use in self-defense. Incredibly, Ahimelech responded, "The sword of Goliath the Philistine, whom you killed in the valley of Elah, behold, it is wrapped in a cloth behind the ephod; if you would take it for yourself, take it. For there is no other except it here." And David said, "There is none like it; give it to me" (21:9).

David should have remembered that this weapon had not delivered Goliath! Why should he now think that it would deliver him? Nevertheless he took Goliath's sword and fled, walking past the valley of Elah where he had fought the giant with his sling. Then he kept going until he came to Gath, the territory from which Goliath had come! He depended on his enemy's sword and his enemy's territory for protection!

Where was the David who had said, "You come to me with a sword, a spear, and a javelin, but I come to you in the name of the Lord of hosts, the God of the armies of Israel, whom you have taunted" (17:45)? His faith in God vanished like dew in the face of the morning sun. In seeking the help of his enemies, David was confessing his lack of trust in the living God.

Often sins that we have previously conquered resurface in our lives. Despair has a way of making us slide into spiritual lethargy so that we give up, questioning whether following God has any practical value. David, the man who thought he had conquered fear, was now controlled by it.

David now took a third step into the moral abyss. In Gath he *lived* a lie! As might be expected, David was instantly recognized in Gath as the man who had killed the mighty giant and so fear flooded his heart. To appear perfectly harmless, he pretended to be a lunatic. "So he disguised his sanity before them, and acted insanely in their hands, and scribbled on the doors of the gate, and let his saliva run down unto his beard. Then Achish said to his servants, 'Behold, you see the man behaving as a madman. Why do you bring him to me? Do I lack madmen, that you have brought this one to act the madman in my presence? Shall this one come into my house?'" (21:13-15).

David's lie appeared to work. The king of the Philistines did not kill this "madman" or take him into custody. The pagans had a custom of ignoring those who were insane, lest the gods be offended. The man after God's own heart scrawled meaninglessly on the walls of the city and let saliva run down his beard. This was an undignified moment in the life of one of God's anointed.

Yet even here David was seeking God. He doubtless felt uncomfortable, praying with the spear of Goliath in one hand while wiping the saliva from his beard with the other. Yet God did not abandon David. Even here the Lord was with him.

We don't know how long David was in Philistine territory, but eventually he escaped to the cave of Adullam, where he was joined by a motley group of friends—who had gathered to form a "resistance movement" to overthrow King Saul. "And everyone who was in distress, and everyone who was in debt, and everyone who was discontented, gathered to him; and he became captain over them. Now there were about four hundred men with him" (22:2). David did not recruit these men, for he had no intention of beginning an organized rebellion against King Saul. They came voluntarily to persuade him to fight for the kingdom.

That, David would not do. He then went to Moab for a time, and returned to Judah. When Saul got wind of his whereabouts, he berated his followers for their failure to keep tabs on David's locations. That was when Doeg, the servant of Saul, in an effort to appease him, told the king how the priest at Nob had assisted David when he came into the tabernacle (v. 9).

Overcome by paranoia, Saul assumed that the whole priesthood was conspiring against him. Ahimelech was called before the king to defend himself, and tried in vain to give the king his own side of the story. Saul told him, "You shall surely die, Ahimelech, you and all your father's household" (v. 16). Thus, because of the "conspiracy," eighty-five priests were unceremoniously put to death. As if that were not sufficient, the whole city of Nob was practically wiped out: "And he struck Nob the city of the priests with the edge of the sword, both men and women, children and infants; also oxen, donkeys, and sheep, he struck with the edge of the sword" (v. 19).

When David heard the news he said to one of Ahimelech's surviving sons, "I knew on that day, when Doeg the Edomite was there,, that he would surely tell Saul. I have brought about the death of every person in your father's household" (v. 22). Of course Saul and not David must be held accountable for the massacre, yet David felt guilty because his trip to the priest was the spark that had lit the fuse of Saul's anger.

Fear had caused David to overreact. Fear made him forget everything he ever knew. Fear made him tell a lie.

David would have been safer in Saul's court, within the will of God, than he was in Philistine territory, outside the will of God. *Whenever we sin to protect ourselves, we are more vulnerable than if we maintain our integrity with God.* To Abraham, who feared retaliation after a decisive military victory, God said, "Do not fear, Abram, I am a shield to you; your reward shall be very great" (Gn 15:1).

Yet, even in this senseless massacre we must see the providential hand of God. Many years before, God had told Eli that he would judge his house by removing it from the priesthood (see 1 Sm 2:31). This slaughter essentially fulfilled that prophecy; and later, when Solomon removed Abiathar from the priesthood, the prophecy was completely fulfilled. What a striking reminder that even when men do evil, they fulfill the word of the Lord!

Our first portrait was of David fleeing in panic. Thankfully, we can now shift our focus to a better picture of him. As we might expect, he came to his senses and returned to his spiritual moorings. And when that happened, he again began to win some victories for God.

David in Prayer

Even during those dark days in the land of the Philistines, David did not forget God. Just as he was leaving Ahimelech to return to Judah, he wrote the words of Psalm 34:

I will bless the Lord at all times;
His praise shall continually be in my mouth.
My soul shall make its boast in the Lord;
The humble shall hear it and rejoice.
O magnify the Lord with me,
And let us exalt His name together.

I sought the Lord, and He answered me,
And delivered me from all my fears. (vv. 1-4)

O taste and see that the Lord is good;
How blessed is the man who takes refuge in Him!
O fear the Lord, you His saints;
For to those who fear Him, there is no want. (vv. 8-9)

The eyes of the Lord are toward the righteous
And His ears are open to their cry. (v. 15)

The Lord is near to the brokenhearted,
And saves those who are crushed in spirit.
Many are the afflictions of the righteous;
But the Lord delivers him out of them all. (vv. 18-19)

The Lord redeems the soul of His servants;
And none of those who take refuge in Him will be condemned. (v. 22)

Notice David learned that trust and fear were mutually exclusive. These opposites cannot coexist in the room of the soul. We cannot have 10 percent trust and 90 percent fear; or even the reverse. There is room for only one of these emotions in our hearts.

Lessons From Failure

There are some important lessons that these two portraits teach us.

First, *even anointed people can fail if they panic rather than pray!* We often face the temptation to act impulsively, to "do what comes naturally" under pressure. But Christ told us that men ought always to pray and not to faint (see Lk 18:1)—giving the distinct impression that we must do one or the other. Either we will pray, or we will be overwhelmed and buckle in the moment of pressure.

No spiritual accomplishment of yesterday can protect us from a serious defeat tomorrow. No matter how many right decisions we have made, just one foolish decision can set forces in motion that will eventually defeat us.

Second, *sin always increases a problem; it does not diminish it.* David told a lie and then went to the Philistines for refuge. And although God graciously preserved him there, he would have been just as safe had he stayed in Judah. God used David's flight to the wilderness to prolong his life; but God did not need David's deceptions or his jaunt into the territory of the enemy to keep him alive.

If sin solves one problem, it will spawn another. Following the will of God is better than turning to sinful deceptions to steer our way through a series of barricades. Let's let God handle the consequences of our obedience!

Later, in desperation, David will backslide again, returning to Philistine territory with his wives and six hundred men. This time God will discipline him, and he will encounter one of the most unbearable experiences in his long and painful ordeal as a fugitive. Each time backsliding becomes easier, but each time God's discipline is more severe.

Third, *where failure abounds, grace abounds much more.* God did not forsake David when he crossed the border into Philistine territory. The Lord was with him despite his doubts, his deceit, and even his feigned insanity. Right there in the middle of his despair, David was reminded of the loving-kindness of God.

When we are in need, we can write a check on the bank of God's grace.

Stuart Hamblen wrote:

It is no secret what God can do
What He's done for others
He'll do for you
With arms wide open
He'll pardon you
It is no secret
What God can do.

David was learning that the God who was with him in his conflict with Saul could calm the troubled waters of his soul. God knew the whereabouts of both Saul and David, and His will was being accomplished.

Unbelief comes more naturally than trust, but only trust lets us rest in the providential care of God.

Chapter Five

Conflict With a Fool
(Read 1 Samuel 25)

An architect worked for an employer who was short on money, but long on faith that business would eventually improve, and they would make a handsome profit. Meanwhile, because of present cash-flow problems, the employer asked his friend to work with only meager pay. So the architect gave about two years to his boss, working up to seventy hours a week in order to make the business successful. Of course he believed that eventually it would all be worthwhile.

A few satisfied clients led to more expensive projects, all done by this energetic employee. Yet though his boss was now making an excellent profit, he simply fired his friend and told him not to expect any back pay. In fact, the employer denied ever having promised his colleague more money than the pittance he had received. The books showed that the architect had made his boss several hundred thousand dollars, but he didn't get any of it. So much for fairness! So much for friendship!

Of course, we would argue that this employee should hire an attorney and fight for what is rightfully his. That might work in the Western world, but we forget that in most countries such an appeal to law is impossible. Even if there were affordable attorneys, the court systems are often corrupt, and the route to justice is littered with insurmountable barricades. So what do you do when you don't have legal options? What does justice look like when the law is taken into one's own hands? A story in the life of David gives us a vivid picture of raw justice.

Back in David's time, there were no legal structures for settling business disputes. A handshake sealed most deals, and a man's word was supposed to be his bond. Injustice, when it occurred, had to be settled by the sword. In the end, it wasn't who was right but who was strongest that prevailed.

When David was running from Saul, the six hundred men who accompanied him needed food and shelter to stay alive. David felt this responsibility keenly and did whatever he could to make friends who would help him through these times of need. In his wanderings, David and his men helped a wealthy man named Nabal (the word means *fool*) who had one thousand goats and three thousand sheep. David's men had frequently protected Nabal's flocks, and had never tried to take advantage of him (1 Sm 25:14-17).

Now David, faced with a need for daily provisions, sent ten of his young men to ask Nabal for some food. "Go up to Carmel, visit Nabal and greet him in my name; and thus you shall say, 'Have a long life, peace be to you, and peace be to your house, and peace be to all that you have'" (vv. 5-6). As David's men approached Nabal, they reminded him of the protection they had afforded him in the past months.

Then they delivered David's request: "Therefore let my young men find favor in your eyes, for we have come on a festive day. Please give whatever you find at hand to your servants and to your son David" (v. 8).

The petition was reasonable and diplomatic because (1) it

did not specify any amount Nabal was to give, but asked "whatever" he would think appropriate; and, (2) David and his men had given Nabal a considerable amount of help. This was confirmed by one of Nabal's servants who later said of David's men, "They were a wall to us both by night and by day, all the time we were with them tending the sheep" (v. 16). Also, (3) David humbled himself, saying that he was Nabal's servant and even his "son."

Sweet reasonableness did not work, however. Nabal greeted the request with utter contempt, "Who is David? And who is the son of Jesse? There are many servants today who are each breaking away from his master. Shall I then take my bread and my water and my meat that I have slaughtered for my shearers, and give it to men whose origin I do not know?" (vv. 10-11).

Obviously, Nabal knew who David was. After all, David had gained national fame as the wonder boy who slew Goliath; he was the man who played the harp in the king's palace, and was known as a fugitive wandering in the hills to escape from a paranoid king. Pride, power, and wealth filled Nabal with derision. This was his opportunity to stomp an important man into the dirt.

Nabal should have been grateful, not just for David's help but also because David had spared the nation from the Philistines. As Keith Kaynor put it, "Everything Nabal owned had been riding on the stone in David's sling some years before" (*When God Chooses,* Regular Baptist Press, 1989, 112). The Philistines might have taken over most of the land if Goliath had triumphed. Yet Nabal acted as though he owed David nothing.

Put yourself in David's shoes: How would you have responded? If you were the king-in-waiting, the anointed of the Lord, and if you were tired and angry, what would you have done? You feel responsible for helping those who have risked their lives to roam with you as an animal among the hills. Now you have been grossly insulted.

Regardless of what our response would have been, David became livid with anger and set out to "even the score" on his own terms. Anger clouded his ability to reason; he chose to follow his emotions. He commanded his men to go with him to kill Nabal and his servants!

This was justice gone mad.

The Response of Retaliation

Samuel had just died, and all Israel had mourned his passing (1 Sm 25:1). Soon after, David went to the wilderness of Paran. And that's when he had this encounter with Nabal. The years of hunger and fear had taken their toll. This insult by a fool pushed him over the brink.

Even if Israel had been governed by laws, David did not have a solid case. What law says that Nabal owed him anything just because he had provided some protection along the way? David could only appeal to the hospitality customs of the Middle East, where one good turn deserves another. There was no rational way to resolve this dispute.

Of course, he could have committed the matter to God, taken his lumps, and hoped to get food elsewhere. After all, there just might be some unexpected provisions along the way. If God was with David, we might expect this "Sweet Psalmist of Israel" to commit his way to God, and go merrily back to his hiding place.

Not this time. David was not always given to great faith. He could win a spiritual battle on a Monday and lose it on a Thursday. Unfortunately, we have so romanticized David that we forget he often responded in all too human and disappointing ways. This was not his finest hour.

In hot anger, David told four hundred of his men to take their swords and avenge the humiliation they had just endured. Two hundred of the men followed David, the other two hundred stayed with the baggage. David was thirsting for blood, intending to wipe out Nabal and slaughter all of his men.

How could David possibly justify the wanton murder of a man and his servants simply because this fool had contemptuously humiliated him? Inflamed anger often leads to a form of retaliation which seeks lopsided justice. The desire for revenge, if not extinguished, can lead to an outburst that can even destroy the innocent. This was a serious case of literal *overkill.*

Equally obvious is the fact that David was not trusting God. Faith would dictate that David entrust his case to the Almighty. There were moments, however, when David did not follow the path of faith but the path of manipulation and pride. This was David taking on himself responsibilities that are best left with God.

Why was David so patient with Saul but so impatient with Nabal? Despite all of Saul's faults, he was yet "the anointed of the Lord." David knew that if he killed the king it would appear that he did it just to speed up his own accession to the throne. David, remember, understood that the kingdom was the Lord's and only God had the right to change its leadership.

Nabal was another matter. He was nothing but a rich fool

whom David now longed to murder. Saul was above David in authority; Nabal was beneath him. Patience with Saul, yes. Patience with Nabal, never!

Yet God graciously protected David from this bizarre act.

The Response of Reason

After David began his journey to Carmel to slaughter Nabal, a young man went to Abigail, Nabal's wife, and told her what he had overheard. He told her that David's men had indeed been good to them, providing a wall of protection night and day. Furthermore, he suspected that David was planning evil against them because of Nabal's disdainful reply.

Abigail was apparently as wise as Nabal was stupid. The Bible tells us, "And the woman was intelligent and beautiful in appearance, but the man was harsh and evil in his dealings, and he was a Calebite" (1 Sm 25:3). To her everlasting credit, Abigail acted immediately: "Then Abigail hurried and took two hundred loaves of bread and two jugs of wine and five sheep already prepared and five measures of roasted grain and a hundred clusters of raisins and two hundred cakes of figs, and loaded them on donkeys" (v. 18). Then without telling her husband, she took some young men with her to meet David along the path.

When she saw David, Abigail dismounted and bowed her head to the ground. Falling at David's feet, she pleaded, "On me alone, my lord, be the blame. And please let your maidservant speak to you, and listen to the words of your maidservant. Please do not let my lord pay attention to this worthless man, Nabal, for as his name is, so is he. Nabal is his name and folly is with him; but I your maidservant did not see the young men of my lord whom you sent" (vv. 24-25).

Then followed a plea that David would accept her gifts as a token of appreciation, and that he would not do the harm that was planned. What is more, she begged David to change his mind so that when he (David) eventually became king, this episode of bloodshed would not be on his record. She ended with a personal request: "When the Lord shall deal well with my lord, then remember your maidservant" (v. 31).

Notice the following: Abigail (1) shrewdly took full responsibility, though she had had nothing to do with the response of her foolish husband. This would make it more difficult (if not impossible) for David to continue to blame Nabal for the incident. Then, she (2) acknowledged that her husband had lived up to his name; in a word, he was a *fool.* Disrespect? Perhaps, but then, it does appear that her analysis was quite correct. Finally, she (3) called David her lord, and acknowledged that he would some day be king of Israel. Whether or not she knew that David had been privately anointed by Samuel, she did know that he was destined for greatness. The rumor that David was to be the next king had spread throughout the land.

As he listened, David saw his own foolishness for what it was. He confessed he had been in error and was on the verge of making a disastrous mistake. "Blessed be the Lord God of Israel, who sent you this day to meet me, and blessed be your discernment, and blessed be you, who have kept me this day from bloodshed, and from avenging myself by my own hand" (vv. 32-33).

David admitted that if Abigail had not intervened he would have killed Nabal and all of his men. Then he received her gifts with this assurance: "Go up to your house in peace. See, I have listened to you and granted your request" (v. 35). Thankfully, this terrible crime would not appear on David's resumé.

The story is not yet over. Abigail returned to her home and did not immediately tell her husband of her successful mission to avert the disaster. In fact, when she returned home her husband was drunk at a feast and so she did not tell him her story until morning. When he heard the details, "His heart died within him so that he became as a stone. And about ten days later, it happened that the Lord struck Nabal, and he died" (vv. 37-38).

David, who had an eye for beautiful women, rejoiced for two reasons; the second was likely more important than the first. First, justice had been served. David was glad that the Lord did what he himself was about to do, namely, kill this fool. Second, he immediately proposed to Abigail and she accepted. She humbly agreed to marry David, saying that she was not even worthy to wash the feet of David's servant. Nevertheless, she went quickly on a donkey to the place where he was and became his wife.

God had graciously intervened in David's life. He had the maturity to realize that if he had carried out his plans he would have had a blot on his reputation that would have haunted him for the rest of his life. And because it is easier to sin the second time, it may well be that he would have often resorted to violence rather than trust in God.

The Response of Faith

How should David have reacted to Nabal in the first place? Obviously, he was wrong in planning retaliation, but what should he have done? And what is there for us to learn about responding to the injustices of life?

This story contains several lessons in resolving disputes. First, *anger causes us to lose perspective.* Uncontrolled anger is always irrational, and though it seeks justice, it becomes a miscarriage of justice. Listen to the words of James: "Let everyone be quick to hear, slow to speak and slow to anger; for the anger of man does not achieve the righteousness of God" (Jas 1:19-20). Please note: *The anger of man does not bring about the righteousness of God.*

Two mistakes are made when we take justice into our own hands. First, we tend to overreact, because of wounded pride or an uncontrolled desire for vengeance. Second, we simply do not have all the facts. We misread intentions, we fail to see our own faults, and we don't see the future. That's why God alone is qualified to rectify the balance of justice for all the evil done on Planet Earth. We can be sure that the judge of all the earth will do right (see Gn 18:25).

When Christ's messengers were rejected by the citizens of Samaria, James and John asked, "'Lord, do You want us to command fire to come down from heaven and consume them?' But He turned and rebuked them" (Lk 9:54-55).

Uncontrolled anger brings destruction, not reconciliation.

Second, *our initial response should be to lay our anger before God.* David acted quickly, willing to do whatever his white-hot temper dictated. A few minutes in the presence of the Almighty might have given him the same kind of levelheaded perspective that Abigail gave him. There in the presence of the Lord, David just might have gotten his bearings and found a more measured response.

Most of us have never seriously thought about murdering someone in the interest of justice; but if we hate our brother, we are guilty of murder in our heart. God not only wants to take the gun from our hand, He also wants to take the poison out of our heart.

God has many resources at his disposal to resolve disputes. He has the power of life and death. As for Nabal, we read, "The Lord struck Nabal, and he died." God caused Nabal to die of natural causes (most likely a heart attack), but behind this common physical ailment was God's providential intervention. Blessed is the person who knows that "our times are in God's hands," and that whatever happens to us has divine authorization.

God can also give us rest, the calm assurance that we can leave our injustices with Him. There is such a thing as fully trusting God to be our avenger. In a calmer moment, David himself wrote, "The Lord lives, and blessed be my rock; and exalted be the God of my salvation, the God who executes vengeance for me, and subdues peoples under me. He delivers me from my enemies; surely Thou dost lift me above those who rise up against me; Thou dost rescue me from the violent man" (Ps 18:46-48).

Paul wrote, "Never take your own revenge, beloved, but leave room for the wrath of God, for it is written, 'Vengeance is Mine, I will repay,' says the Lord" (Rom 12:19).

David and Paul are agreed: God will vindicate us in His own time; we are to believe this and act accordingly.

Third, *we must look at injustice through the eyes of the cross.* David could not have this perspective, of course, but we can.

Where is justice? We cry when we see wrongs that are unanswered, acts that go unpunished. Peter tells us what Christ did when He was falsely accused: "And while being reviled, He did not revile in return; while suffering, He uttered no threats, but kept entrusting Himself to Him who judges righteously" (1 Pt 2:23). Christ did not retaliate because He knew that this injustice was only temporary. Eventually, this case would be meticulously reviewed by the Supreme Court. Justice was coming.

We can forgive those who have wronged us without surrendering our desire for justice. We must simply realize that our case may not be tried immediately. But be assured, it *will* be tried—by God Himself. Eventually the truth will come out, and justice will be meted out with fairness. The wicked will continue to prey on the righteous. The wealthy will exploit the poor. Some employers will continue to chisel employees out of what is their due. And some parents will continue to be cruel to their children.

What do you say to the person who has been cheated out of the money that is due him? Or the one who is the victim of cruel lies and even violence? To such we must say, "God has entrusted you with the same kind of suffering that His Son endured." To be treated unjustly is to follow most fully in the footsteps of Christ.

Let us do what we can to rectify this world's wrongs; let us use whatever means our culture has available to defend the oppressed and punish the guilty. But let us also accept the cruel fact that multiplied millions of injustices will never be made right, and that our earthly quest for justice will always fall short.

David might have returned a second time to Nabal, to once more reason with this fool. Or he might have taken it a step further and demanded payment with the threat of the sword. Or he might have simply committed his complaint to God, trusting the Almighty to vindicate him and supply the needed food. Any of these options would have been better than what he had planned.

Thankfully, God often intervenes to keep us from sin. Every day we should pray, "O God, when I desire to do wrong, may I not have the opportunity; and when I have the opportunity, may I not have the desire!" Without God's restraint, many of us might have ruined our lives and reputations long ago.

Some conflicts we can resolve; others are best left with God. Both kinds will be meticulously retried in the ages to come.

Chapter Six

Conflict Within the Soul
(Read 1 Samuel 26-30)

If you like butterflies, you will have to like cocoons.

We've been taught to think of David as a great man of faith, worship, and music, a man who spent his life delighting the heart of God. That may be David the butterfly; we forget that many times he was David the cocoon. David the defeated, discouraged rebel.

One day, while living in enemy territory, David slid down a rope only to find that there was no knot at the end. The disillusionment was so deep he simply did not know where to turn. In that predicament, he illustrates *what we can do when we don't know what to do.* There is always one step left to take.

A friend of mine said that when his wife left him for another man, he went to bed at night hoping he would not wake up in the morning. A mother who discovered that her son was a homosexual felt so crushed that she stopped praying, thinking she had been abandoned by God. A man whose wife and daughter were killed in a plane crash committed suicide, leaving a note: "Marilyn and Ruthie will need me on the other side; I can't go on without them."

If you are wondering how you can manage for one more day, you have a friend in David. He painted himself into a corner, with no path leading out. Yet, at the end of his extremity he found God.

What got David into this terrible mess? He failed in some weak moments and found himself in desperate circumstances. He listened to his fears rather than to his faith. And when he fell he dragged a host of others into his predicament.

We all know that God had replaced Goliath with Saul in David's school of brokenness. In chapter 4 we learned that, in a moment of discouragement, David went into the territory of the Philistines to escape from the mad king. He returned to Judah but under increasing pressure and fear retreated to the Philistines and actually joined their army. There he encountered one of the darkest moments of his life.

David's descent into the abyss of despair was a gradual process, the result of years of pressure and fear. There are several reasons why David became weak—physically, morally, and spiritually. Here is the story.

Weakened by Discouragement

Let's recap why David was so discouraged: When Saul heard that David was hiding in the caves among the hills, he took three thousand of his best men to search for him, absolutely determined to kill his potential rival. David's spies informed their leader about Saul's movements; in fact, they even knew exactly where Saul and his bodyguards had camped. David saw the place where Saul lay, surrounded by his choicest men.

Incredibly, David had the nerve to suggest that he and a few friends go down to the camp while Saul and his men were sleeping. Abishai agreed, begging David's permission to kill this evil king who had brought so much heartache to so many. This, Abishai said, is a God-given opportunity: "Today God has delivered your enemy into your hand; now therefore, please let me strike him with the spear to the ground" (1 Sm 26:8).

David begged to differ. He interpreted this opportunity as a test of faith. Only God had the right to get rid of the king, at his own time and in his own way. "Do not destroy him, for who can stretch out his hand against the Lord's anointed and be without guilt?... As the Lord lives, surely the Lord will strike him ... or he will go down into battle and perish. The Lord forbid that I should stretch out my hand against the Lord's anointed" (vv. 9-11). The kingdom is the Lord's!

So, rather than killing the sleeping Saul, David took the spear and jug of water that were lying beside his head, and quietly left. Why didn't any of Saul's party awaken, as David and Abishai crept among them? We read, "But no one saw or knew it, nor did any awake, for they were all asleep, because a sound sleep from the Lord had fallen on them" (v. 12).

After David had climbed far above the encampment, he taunted Saul and Abner, his chief bodyguard. He shouted to Abner, "Are you not a man? And who is like you in Israel? Why then have you not guarded your lord the king? For one of the people came to destroy the king your lord" (v. 15). Then David showed Abner Saul's spear and the jug of water!

Saul recognized David's voice; they were close enough to shout to each other. David asked Saul why he was trying to kill him, and begged the king to stop his murderous pursuit, "For the king of Israel has come out to search for a single flea, just as one hunts a partridge in the mountains" (v. 20).

Saul was humiliated. He confessed that he had sinned, and assured David that he would never seek him again. "I have sinned. Return, my son David, for I will not harm you again because my life was precious in your sight this day. Behold, I have played the fool and have committed a serious error" (v. 21). David made the point that, just as he valued Saul's life, Saul should now return the favor and value his. The spear and the jug were a sign of David's loyalty. Saul responded, "Blessed are you, my son David; you will both accomplish much and surely prevail" (v. 25).

If you were David, would you have believed Saul? How much faith can you put in a man who has repented numerous times but has always returned to his former ways? Can you believe a man possessed by a murderous spirit? Can you believe a man who would ask three thousand men to comb the countryside just to find a young man who had done him no harm?

David was shrewd enough to know that the answer was no. Wisdom dictated that he would have to continue to be a man on the run. He was weary of living in the wild, running from cave to cave. His discouragement had eroded his faith in the God who had anointed him and protected him all these years.

Though David was courageous in tiptoeing into Saul's camp at night, he was not courageous enough to believe that God could protect him in the familiar hills of Bethlehem. The victory of yesterday did not sustain him today. Rather than running to the hills of Judah, he ran in the opposite direction, right into the territory occupied by the enemies of God.

This was a conscious decision to do what he thought was best, without consulting God.

Weakened by Backsliding

David decided that he could best confuse Saul by again running to the Philistines and living with them. "Now I will perish one day by the hand of Saul. There is nothing better for me than to escape into the land of the Philistines. Saul then will despair of searching for me any more in all the territory of Israel, and I will escape from his hand" (1 Sm 27:1).

So David and six hundred of his supporters took up residence with Achish, king of Gath, in whose presence he had previously feigned insanity. In fact, King Achish even gave David and his men the city of Ziklag. When we turn to the world for refuge, the enemy of our souls is only too happy to make us comfortable!

From time to time David and his men would raid other tribes in the area, such as the Geshurites and the Girzites and the Amalekites. These tribes were descendants of the Canaanites whom God had told Joshua to destroy. David, no doubt, felt that these massacres were sanctioned by God.

But when King Achish asked where these raids were conducted, David lied to him: "Against the Negev of Judah and against the Negev of the Jerahmeelites and against the Negev of the Kenites" (v. 10). He told the king that he had been fighting against Judah, just to make himself look good to these pagans. Lies, David, lies!

Achish believed David, saying, "He has surely made himself odious among his people Israel; therefore he will become my servant forever" (v. 12). The king had a right to boast of the new alliance that was formed with David, one of the most famous leaders of Israel. All on the king's terms!

Here is the final irony: The Philistines were going to war against Israel, and David and his men were expected to join their army! David might have known that the Philistines would soon cash in their IOUs. One favor deserves another. If David and his men were allowed to live with the Philistines, they owed them help when they went to war. There is no such thing as free protection and free rent. *If you live with us, fight with us.*

The invitation to fight in the Philistine army was given and accepted. And as if that were not enough, Achish the king asked David to be his bodyguard, and David said, "Very well, you shall know what your servant can do." So Achish said to David, "Very well, I will make you my bodyguard for life" (28:2).

Although Achish believed David was loyal to the Philistine cause, some of his generals had their doubts. So David was sent back from the front lines.

Incredibly, David objected and asked the king, "But what have I done? And what have you found in your servant from the day when I came before you to this day, that I may not go and fight against the enemies of my lord the king?" (29:8). Was David sincerely asking that he be allowed to fight? Or was this a ploy to keep himself in good standing with the king?

Whatever his motive, the man who had slain Goliath the Philistine was now volunteering to go to war with the Philistines against Israel! Some commentators have given David the benefit of the doubt and assumed that, if he had gone to battle, he and his men would have become traitors and joined the battle against the Philistines on behalf of Israel. Regardless, David was hopelessly out of place. What a predicament for a servant of God!

Here is a lesson for all of us: Whenever we side with the enemy of our souls, he always makes us feel welcome and even gives us a place that we can call our own. But later we will be expected to fight with him against the people of God. Every inch of territory we give to the world will pressure us to give one more. Satan's goal is to make us enemies of the God who loves us.

Some Christians find themselves fighting in the wrong army. To side with our adversary is simple enough: We only need to serve two masters; we just need to stand on the territory that belongs to the world. James wrote, "You adulteresses, do you not know that friendship with the world is hostility toward God? Therefore whoever wishes to be a friend of the world makes himself an enemy of God" (Jas 4:4). Imagine a child of God adopting the values and attitudes of God's enemy!

Surely David would never have dreamed he would be willing to become a traitor to God and His people. But then, no one who flirts with the world ever intends to be overcome by it; no person who wastes his life ever begins with that as his goal. Backsliding is taking a series of small, comfortable decisions, with the full intention of controlling the consequences. Only later do we lose our footing and slide into the swamp we always thought we would avoid.

David's backsliding weakened his ability to trust God. And discipline from God was just around the corner.

Weakened by Sorrow

When David returned to Ziklag, he discovered to his horror that everything he had left behind had been destroyed by the Amalekites, a warring tribe bent on plunder and revenge. The city itself was burned; worse, "They took captive the women and all who were in it, both small and great, without killing anyone, and carried them off and went their way" (1 Sm 30:1-2).

When David and his men discovered the city was burned and that their wives and children had been taken captive, they "lifted their voices and wept until there was no strength in them to weep" (v. 4). Of course at this time they did not know whether their families were dead or alive. As far as David and his men were concerned they were widowers, for the Amalekites were cruel people who often killed those they had conquered. And since one evil turn deserves another, such a slaughter would have been easily justified—because David had done the same to them (27:8-9). Little wonder David and his men wept until they had no strength left.

Weakened by Rejection

To make matters worse, David's friends now contemplated stoning him. "Moreover David was greatly distressed because the people spoke of stoning him, for all the people were embittered, each one because of his sons and daughters" (1 Sm 30:6). The people knew that all of this was, to a large degree, David's fault. It was his idea to try to "hide" in Philistine territory. It was his idea to raid the warring tribes who were seeking revenge. Worse, it was his idea to agree to go to battle against Israel, leaving the wives and families vulnerable to an attack. David, a military man, should have known better.

David felt this responsibility with all the pain his body could bear. To face the death of his own wives was one thing; to bear the sorrow of all his men was too much. These were the men who had risked their lives for him in his flight from Saul. He had not only brought destruction upon himself but also on those whom he loved. He could understand why even his loyal friends contemplated stoning him.

David was a king without a throne; a husband without a wife; a leader without followers; a believer without a witness. This was his reward for ten years of wandering, ten years of trusting God to fulfill His promise. That day he was anointed in Bethlehem was a distant memory that now seemed like a charade. Where was this God who chose him to be king? Why did the Almighty say He had rejected Saul if He still allowed him to rule for another ten years? Why did the whole nation have to suffer under the hand of this deranged schizophrenic? Could God really be trusted to fulfill His promises?

David knew that this was the judgment of God. He should have known that he would not be safe in enemy territory, no matter how much he had come to trust Achish, king of Gath. He should have remembered that God could have protected him without his resorting to the help of pagans.

What did David do when there was nothing left to do? We read, "David strengthened himself in the Lord his God" (v. 6). At last he looked up rather than within; at last he sought the only One who could save him. With no options left, there in the presence of the Almighty he became reacquainted with the One whom he had come to love. He poured out his soul to the only friend who would understand, and found the strength to go on. With God's enablement he could face tomorrow.

What strength did David receive when he cast himself upon the mercy of God?

Strengthened by God

David's first need was for *spiritual* strength and communion with God. He said to Abiathar the priest, "Please bring me the ephod" (1 Sm 30:7). "And David inquired of the Lord, saying, 'Shall I pursue this band? Shall I overtake them?' And He said to him, 'Pursue, for you shall surely overtake them, and you shall surely rescue all'" (v. 8).

When David called, God answered!

David sought God for wisdom, something he should have done months before. In humiliation he returned to fellowship with the God he had left in his days of unbelief. Yes, there is a kind of sorrow that works repentance. For some the valley of trouble is the door of hope.

How wonderful it was for David to hear God's voice again! God was willing to talk when David was ready to listen. The word from the Lord said that David should pursue the enemy and overtake them.

When we are out of fellowship with God, what trials must come to bring us back? How much grief has to come our way before we begin to listen to God again? For every mile the

Prodigal Son walked away from his father's house, he had a mile to return. Time spent out of fellowship with God can be forgiven, but it can never be regained. David's defection would not be held against him, but some scars would remain.

How long does it take us to get back into fellowship with God, after we become conscious that we have sinned? How much discomfort do we have to feel before we return to God after failure and sin? A mark of spiritual maturity is to keep short accounts with God; that is, we should not allow sin to accumulate. We will not find ourselves wandering in the enemy territory if we stay in fellowship with God all the time.

When David was desperate, the spiritual strength was granted.

Second, he received *moral* strength. He convinced his men not to stone him, but to join a search mission to retrieve their families. He could not lose precious time wallowing in shame. Nor was there any use trying to project blame on anyone else. He did not say that it was the Amalekites' fault, even though everyone knew that they were responsible for their own cruelty. Nor did David blame his generals, who should have had the good sense to protect the city when they left for battle. Achish the king could have been the target of David's anger for inviting him to join the Philistines in the first place. But David took the blame.

This was not the time for clever games, hedging responsibility. He was their leader; he had led them into this difficulty, and he was not about to shirk responsibility or make excuses.

So David left with the six hundred men. Two hundred came only a short distance to guard whatever remained of home base. Then he went with the remaining four hundred. Providentially, they found a young Egyptian who had been a part of the Ziklag raid; he told David where the Amalekites were camped. "And when he had brought him down, behold, they were spread over all the land, eating and drinking and dancing because of all the great spoil that they had taken from the land of the Philistines and from the land of Judah" (v. 16). David and his men crashed the party, killing all the Amalekites except four hundred young men who fled on camels. They recovered all the loot, and their wives and children.

When David returned to the two hundred men who had stayed behind, some of the four hundred who had gone into battle complained: "Because they did not go with us, we will not give them any of the spoil that we have recovered, except to every man his wife and his children, that they may lead them away and depart" (v. 22).

David chided them for their selfishness: "For as his share is who goes down to the battle, so shall his share be who stays by the baggage; they shall share alike" (v. 24). This became a statute in Israel: *Those who stay to guard the equipment share the victory with those who have won the battle.* David's dependence on God had renewed his moral strength.

Third, David even received *physical* strength. He had to pursue the Amalekites to recover the families and the goods. Though emotionally weak, he was physically strong to follow the instructions of the Lord. *God gives us the strength to do whatever he commands.*

Out of his grief, David wrote words that can comfort the most desperate heart:

The cords of death encompassed me, and the torrents of ungodliness terrified me. The cords of Sheol surrounded me; the snares of death confronted me. In my distress I called upon the Lord, and cried to my God for help; He heard my voice out of His temple, and my cry for help before Him came into His ears.

PSALM 18:4-6

The cocoon produced the butterfly. Backsliding eventually led to blessing.

David's lesson is summarized in the words of a Puritan who said that *those who have God and everything else do not have more than those who have God only!* Or, to put it differently, when we have nothing left but God, we can discover that God is enough.

In that lonely moment on the cross, Jesus cried, "My God, My God ... why hast Thou forsaken Me?" We will never have to utter that question. Even when we have come to the end of our rope, we still have God. "'I will never desert you, nor will I ever forsake you,' so that we confidently say, 'The Lord is my helper, I will not be afraid. What shall man do to me?'" (Heb 13:5-6).

There *is* something you can do when you don't know what to do. God still strengthens those who are too weak to face tomorrow.

Chapter Seven

Conflict With Grief
(Read 1 Samuel 31; 2 Samuel 1-3)

Perhaps you have read C.S. Lewis' book, *A Grief Observed,* the story of his wife's slow death from cancer. With increasing pain Lewis watched his wife grow weaker. Within three years of their wedding she died. The opening words of the book are, "Nobody ever told me."

No matter how much may be said about grief, we are never ready when tragedy strikes. Though we read accounts of others whose loved ones die, we cannot understand what it is like until we pass through the valley of sorrow for ourselves. Lewis wrote, "Nobody ever told me how much grief was like fear."

Our world is filled with grief. Some mourn the loss of a loved one; others the loss of a marriage or of good health. Millions grieve because of famine, earthquakes, or the devastation of disease. Ours is a world of sorrow.

Grief itself is not all bad. In fact, if handled correctly it can be God's way of preparing us to enter into a new phase of existence. Yet, improperly handled, sorrow can be devastating. Some people become locked into the past and never make the transition to new challenges and relationships. *Good* grief should help us face our sorrow and clarify our values. What we *believe* determines how *we grieve.*

When David mourns the deaths of Saul and Jonathan, the curtain lifts and we have an intimate glimpse into his soul. The conflict with Saul is over; the friendship with Jonathan is past. It is time to mourn, to contemplate the past, and to think of what might have been. It is also a time to think about tomorrow.

The Experience of Shock

Even when the death of a loved one is expected, the news always comes with an air of finality; there is a profound feeling of permanent loss. Some cry uncontrollably, others cannot cry at all. Others become angry, lashing out at God or even the dead one who has left them in loneliness.

Let's review the way in which Saul and Jonathan died. Recall that the Philistines had prepared for war against Israel, and the battle was concentrated at Mount Gilboa. There Jonathan was killed along with his brothers. As for Saul, we read, "And the battle went heavily against Saul, and the archers hit him; and he was badly wounded by the archers. Then Saul said to his armor bearer, 'Draw your sword and pierce me through with it, lest these uncircumcised come and pierce me through and make sport of me'" (1 Sm 31:3-4).

But the armor bearer did not have the courage to kill the king. So Saul committed suicide by falling on his own spear. And when the armor bearer saw that Saul was dead, he also fell on his sword and committed suicide.

The next day the Philistines discovered the bodies of Saul and his three sons. They cut off Saul's head, stripped off his weapons, and sent them throughout the land of the Philistines to carry the good news to their people so that they might give thanks to their gods. Then they hung Saul's body and that of Jonathan on the wall of the city of Bethshan (v. 10). The inhabitants of Jabesh-gilead took the bodies by night and burned them and buried their bones at Jabesh.

News of the deaths reached David just after he had gone to retrieve his wives from the raid of the Amalekites. A man came out of the camp of Saul with his clothes torn and dust on his head. He fell to the ground before David and told him that Jonathan and Saul were dead.

The young man told his story:

By chance I happened to be on Mount Gilboa, and behold, Saul was leaning on his spear. And behold, the chariots and the horsemen pursued him closely. And when he looked behind him, he saw me and called to me. And I said, "Here I am." And he said to me, "Who are you?" and I answered him, "I am an Amalekite." Then he said to me, "Please stand beside me and kill me; for agony has seized me because my life still lingers in me." So I stood beside him and killed him, because I knew that he could not live after he had fallen. And I took the crown which was on his head and the bracelet which was on his arm, and I have brought them here to my lord.

2 SAMUEL 1:6-10

David, who had spent several years in Saul's court, could positively identify the crown and the bracelet, which appeared to confirm the man's story. When news of a death strikes, we instinctively wonder whether there has been a mistake, either in communication or identification. When David saw this jewelry, he knew Saul was dead.

He expressed shock. Consistent with Middle Eastern expressions of grief, we read, "Then David took hold of his clothes and tore them, and so also did all the men who were with him. And they mourned and wept and fasted until evening for Saul and his son Jonathan and for the people of the Lord and the house of Israel, because they had fallen by the sword" (vv. 11-12).

Scholars, however, are divided as to whether this young man was telling the truth about his involvement in Saul's death. Since we read in 1 Samuel 31:4 that Saul fell on his sword and committed suicide, it is unlikely that this Amalekite actually killed the fallen king. More likely, he came by and saw that Saul was dead and stole the crown and the bracelet from his body. He embellished the account to make himself look like a hero.

But he told the story to the wrong man! He expected to be honored for killing David's enemy, but discovered to his horror that David commanded him to be executed. David asked him, "How is it you were not afraid to stretch out your hand to destroy the Lord's anointed?" (2 Sm 1:14).

David was practically obsessed with the firm conviction that the kingdom belonged to God and no man had the right to usurp that authority. Apparently he thought that even this Amalekite should have known that Saul was "God's anointed." Since David himself would not touch the Lord's anointed, he was angry that someone else had the audacity to do so.

Politically, this was also a shrewd move, for it was a signal to those loyal to Saul that David would have no part in manipulating his way to the throne. David made it clear that he did not rejoice in the death of the king who had been his mortal enemy. Whatever we may think of David's snap judgment, the young man was promptly executed.

When we hear the news of the death of a friend or relative our first response is shock, a sense of disbelief. Some people become angry with the doctor; others are filled with disbelief or fear. Our emotions become numb; for some there are tears, others cannot cry. During those first few hours and days there may be disorientation, difficulty in adjusting to reality.

David responded with grief and an act of violence.

The Experience of Reflection

Saul, for all of his faults, was the king who had given David permission to fight against the giant, the act that had catapulted David to stardom. David knew Saul well, serving as his court musician and armor bearer.

Jonathan, the king's son, loved David as he loved his own soul. Although Jonathan was legally next in line for the throne, he delighted in the fact that his friend would be the next king. No jealousy, no animosity, just unconditional and caring love. They had made a covenant between themselves that they would love each other until death. Now, Jonathan was dead, and David felt the loss most keenly.

David eulogized the lives of Saul and Jonathan and gave a moving tribute to their greatness and accomplishments. In grief there is often a loss of perspective that makes the mourners idealize the person who has died. David spoke of how Saul and Jonathan were loved, and how beautiful they were together.

First, he expressed concern that their deaths would be greeted with jubilation by Israel's enemies:

> Your beauty, O Israel, is slain on your high places! How have the mighty fallen! Tell it not in Gath, proclaim it not in the streets of Ashkelon; lest the daughters of the Philistines rejoice, lest the daughters of the uncircumcised exult.
>
> 2 SAMUEL 1:19-20

Second, he concentrated on the good memories he had of them, overlooking Saul's folly. As A.W. Pink says, "Forgetting the mad hatred and relentless persecution of his late enemy, thinking of the friendship of his earlier days and his official status of the anointed of the Lord... [David] cast over the mangled corpses of Saul and Jonathan the mantle of his noble elegy in which he sings the praise of the one and celebrates the love of the other" (*The Life of David,* vol. 1, Reiner Publishing, 1969, 235).

David continued:

> Saul and Jonathan, beloved and pleasant in their life, and in their death they were not parted; they were swifter than eagles, they were stronger than lions.
>
> 2 SAMUEL 1:23

Then follows an especially touching tribute to probably the only man who ever really loved David:

I am distressed for you, my brother Jonathan; you have been very pleasant to me. Your love to me was more wonderful than the love of women. How have the mighty fallen, and the weapons of war perished!

2 SAMUEL 1:26-27

Whatever failures David had experienced in his personal reactions to Saul, he could take heart that he could look back with no regrets. To the end he had remained a loyal subject in Saul's kingdom, supporting his leadership. Only when the spears began to fly did David leave; and even then he left alone. Those who came to him were not recruited, but were volunteers who were frustrated because David refused to capitalize on his opportunities to topple the king.

David now knew that the waiting had been worthwhile.

The Experience of Understanding

David attempted to grapple with ultimate questions; he contemplated the deaths of Jonathan and Saul from God's perspective, trying to fit it into the Almighty's eternal purpose.

Whenever we are faced with death, we seek to answer the question, "Why?" A drunk drives his car into the path of an oncoming car and an innocent couple is killed. A baby dies because his mother used cocaine during the pregnancy. In these and a hundred different scenarios, the fate of the guilty and the innocent are bound together. Our impending death or the death of a friend always confronts us with the mystery of God's ways. We think about eternity, heaven, and hell. We ask whether the past could have been different.

When someone dies today, we are left to draw our own conclusions about the hidden purposes of God. In Saul's case, however, the Scriptures are clear: "So Saul died for his trespass which he committed against the Lord, because of the word of the Lord which he did not keep; and also because he asked counsel of a medium, making inquiry of it, and did not inquire of the Lord. Therefore he killed him, and turned the kingdom to David the son of Jesse" (1 Chr 10:13-14).

Just as God killed Nabal, so also God killed Saul, using the Philistines to accomplish His will. Nabal died of a heart attack; Saul died by the sword; but both died as appointed by God. Their deaths were divine judgment. The lives of the wicked are often cut short when God chooses to end their rebellion. Even in the New Testament, there is "a sin unto death" (1 Jn 5:16).

We know that Saul died at his appointed time, but what about Jonathan? He did not die for his sin, but as the result of his father's rebellion. The human race is inextricably linked, and the righteous die with the wicked. Yes, Jonathan also died at his appointed time. God's providential care of His people takes into account the actions of evil men. For though Jonathan's fate was bound up with his father's, the death of all men is ultimately subject to a divine plan that includes accidents, disease, and war. Even Christ, the victim of the murderous hatred of evil men, died at the appointed time.

David had been through the darkness; soon the sun would shine, but not yet. He felt the sharp sting of pain, the fear and the loss that the death of a friend always brings.

But there would soon be much to do in this new phase of his existence.

The Experience of Rebuilding

Someone has said, "A man can put off making up his mind, but he can't put off making up his life." Time marches on, there is a time to mourn and a time to act; a time to cry and a time to laugh.

Bad grief will not acknowledge that there is life after sorrow. Good grief comes to terms with the full impact of the loss, but it can also grasp that life must continue: As long as one is alive, life is to be lived. A businessman prayed, "O God, keep me alive until I die!"

David now inquired of the Lord as to what the next move was to be. The Lord replied that he should go to the cities of Judah and he would be successful. So he went to Hebron, where he was anointed king over the house of Judah (see 2 Sm 2:1-4). He also thanked the men of Jabesh-gilead for giving Saul and Jonathan a decent burial.

The period of grief had to be cut short because political opposition was developing that needed David's attention. Abner, the son of Ner, who had been Saul's bodyguard, crowned Ishbosheth (Saul's son, whose name means "man of shame") king over the house of Israel. That meant civil war.

So while David was reigning in Hebron over the tribe of Judah, the northern tribes were governed by the fragmented leadership of one of Saul's sons. Ishbosheth and David were not personally involved in the conflict, but left their interests in the hands of their generals. Joab was loyal to David; Abner represented Ishbosheth. Rather than have their entire armies fight, they agreed to have a "contest" at the pool of Gibeon. Twelve men from each faction would fight in single combat to determine a winner. The match was a draw, since all twenty-four were killed (v. 16). Life was cruel in those days!

Meanwhile, Abner incurred the wrath of Joab by killing Joab's brother Asahel. Obviously, the nation could no longer afford to be torn among these warring factions, and Abner was astute enough to realize that he was backing a loser. We read, "Now there was a long war between the house of Saul and the house of David; and David grew steadily stronger, but the house of Saul grew weaker continually" (3:1).

Abner switched his allegiance from Ishbosheth to David, and helped persuade the northern tribes to accept the inevitable. David was destined to be king over the whole land, so there was little use in prolonging the war. Despite this change of heart, Abner was murdered by Joab to avenge the death of Asahel (v. 30). Later Ishbosheth was murdered by some well-meaning supporters of David.

Again, David was not impressed with the zeal of those who killed Saul's son Ishbosheth. David compared their actions with the Amalekite who killed Saul in battle, and asked, "How much more, when wicked men have killed a righteous man in his own house on his bed, shall I not now require his blood from your hand, and destroy you from the earth?" (4:11). David had them executed, because they had killed a righteous man who was defenseless.

With the civil war over and the northern tribes ready to accept David as their king, we read, "So all the elders of Israel came to the king at Hebron, and King David made a covenant with them before the Lord at Hebron; then they anointed David king over Israel. David was thirty years old when he became king, and he reigned forty years" (5:3-4).

Fourteen years had passed since David had been anointed in the midst of his brothers on the outskirts of Bethlehem. For ten of those years he had been a fugitive with nowhere to call home. There in the school of brokenness, he wrote poetry that would become the best tonic for aching hearts. God had proved faithful, but the conflict was not yet over. There was a whole new set of lessons to learn in God's curriculum.

Lessons on Death and Dying

The deaths of Saul and Jonathan remind us that ultimately *only God can evaluate a man's life.* David's praise of Saul was magnanimous, generous, and poetic. But what will God say of Saul? We do not know whether Saul was ever "converted," in the Old Testament sense of that word. We do know that the Holy Spirit came upon him and "God changed his heart" (1 Sm 10:9). Subsequent events gave little evidence of this transformation, but we cannot be certain of his final destiny. Even if he was converted, possibly the king gave himself his own best epitaph when he said, "I have played the fool" (26:21).

In the end, only God is qualified to judge this tormented king. Only God knows why he could not extricate the beast of jealousy from his heart. Only God knows why he found true repentance so difficult. Only God knows why David believed the kingdom was God's and Saul believed the kingdom was his.

As for Jonathan, the adoration given by David might be only a shadow of the approval given to him by the Almighty. Think of the humility of this man who had such a poor example for a father. Yet, we cannot read the thoughts and intents of the heart. We must leave our assessment of Jonathan to God as well.

The deaths of this father and son also teach us that no one is ready to live until he is ready to die. Saul died essentially as he had lived, in rebellion and irrational jealousy. He was, to the end, a vengeful man who was willing to risk both soul and body to kill a young man who had done him no harm. Though he repented five times, it was always a halfhearted response after being shamed into seeing himself for what he was. As soon as the humiliation passed, he reverted to form, back to his satanic blindness.

Those who know that their eternal destiny is with God can afford to live a life of trust on earth. By God's grace we can choose to be a Jonathan rather than a Saul.

Finally, we see that God gave grace in the midst of grief. David found comfort in his sorrow, for God sustained him. Even when Jonathan was alive, he could not always be at David's side. But God could be. He was also there when Jonathan passed off the scene.

"Grief," said C.S. Lewis, "is like fear."

David would have agreed, yet in confidence wrote:

The Lord is my light and my salvation; whom shall I fear?
The Lord is the defense of my life; whom shall I dread?
When evildoers came upon me to devour my flesh, my adversaries and my enemies, they stumbled and fell.

Though a host encamp against me, my heart will not fear; though war arise against me, in spite of this I shall be confident.

PSALM 27:1-3

In a world of change, God is the one constant who is always there when we need Him. Our grief and fears are under His providential control.

Chapter Eight

Conflict With God
(Read 2 Samuel 5-6)

Yes, there are times when we become angry at God.

A man whose wife died of cancer accused God of insensitivity. "God isn't worth a plug nickel to me," he said bitterly. "Where was He when I needed Him?"

A woman was angry because of the abuse she had suffered as a child. "God wasn't there when I needed Him; why should I expect Him to be there for me now?"

The silence of God in the midst of human suffering prompted one angry skeptic to remark, "If God exists, he must be the devil!" Anger at God.

Our anger toward the circumstances of life and toward people usually translates into anger against God. No matter what explanation we have for the evil in the world, back behind starvation, crime, abuse, and pain, is a God who watches and does not intervene. Is He not the ultimate Cause, the one Being in the universe who could put an end to this madness?

David also became angry with God. In the process of telling his story, we will find out how to respond to the anger we might have toward the Almighty. But first we need to review a bit of history to understand the circumstances of his bitter outburst.

The Capture of Jerusalem

David reigned as king in Hebron for seven years and six months. He knew, however, that Jerusalem was to be the capital city and so he and his men went up to capture it. The Jebusites had controlled it ever since the days of Joshua (see Jos 15:63), proof of its security and defensibility.

The Jebusites taunted David, and for good reason—they thought that he could never capture their city. "You shall not come in here, but the blind and the lame shall turn you away," they shouted over the walls (2 Sm 5:6). They could afford to ridicule David, they thought, because they brought water into the city through a secret passage that had been cut out of rock. With this water supply and a food stockpile, the Jebusites believed they could outlast any siege.

David gave his men a challenge: Whoever would be the man to lead the capture of this city, that one would become the leader of his army. Joab, one of David's military leaders, accepted the opportunity to prove his prowess and entered the city through the water tunnel (see 1 Chr 11:6; 2 Sm 5:8). This access probably enabled him to lead some of his troops into the city and throw the gates open to the waiting armies.

Finally, David was at peace, the admired ruler of the land, with his capital in the city chosen by God. We read, "And David became greater and greater, for the Lord God of hosts was with him" (v. 10). Though he immediately found himself with a series of battles against the Philistines, God communicated to him directly, giving him wisdom in how to fight and win the wars.

But he also had to tend to some unfinished business.

Bringing the Ark to Jerusalem

The ark of God, the chest that was placed in the Holy of Holies, had been housed in the tabernacle at Shiloh after the Israelites entered the land under the leadership of Joshua. This box was made of wood covered with gold, and on the lid were carvings of two cherubim facing each other. Four rings were placed on the sides of the ark, and poles were placed through these rings so that the ark could be carried on the shoulders of the priests. This was a sacred piece of furniture, for it symbolized the divine presence, the very glory of God (see Ex 25:22).

This ark (approximately four feet long, two feet wide, and two feet high) was never to be separated from the tabernacle and its furniture. But one day the Israelites, in an act of rebellion, decided to take the ark into battle as a good luck charm against the Philistines. The ark was captured by these pagans, who were promptly judged by God for having it in their territory. Eventually they returned the ark to Israel (see 1 Sm 4-6). It was brought to the inhabitants of Kiriath-jearim (nine miles north of Jerusalem), where it was kept for twenty years (7:1-2).

The time had now come to bring the ark of God to the new permanent capital. David personally led thirty thousand men to Baal-judah (another name for Kiriath-jearim) to retrieve the ark, intending to bring it to Jerusalem with celebration and fanfare (see 2 Sm 6:2).

David was confident he was doing God's will, because (1) God had specifically said that he wanted the ark brought to Jerusalem (see Dt 12:14), and (2) David used the occasion to worship God. When the ark was being carried, we read,

"Meanwhile, David and all the house of Israel were celebrating before the Lord with all kinds of instruments made of fir wood, and with lyres, harps, tambourines, castanets, and cymbals" (2 Sm 6:5). Here we have a high moment of adoration and praise.

David also thought he was taking the utmost care in bringing the sacred box to his new capital. We read, "And they placed the ark of God on a new cart that they might bring it from the house of Abinadab which was on the hill; and Uzzah and Ahio, the sons of Abinadab, were leading the new cart" (v. 3).

Along the way they passed over a rough outcropping of stone at the threshing floor of Nacon; there the oxen stumbled, the cart jolted, and the ark was about to be thrown on the ground. Uzzah, who had grown up with the ark in his home (see 1 Sm 7:1), instinctively reached out to prevent its fall. Then we read, "God struck him down there for his irreverence; and he died there by the ark of God" (2 Sm 6:7). The celebration was interrupted as the stricken man fell with a thud to the ground.

Stunned silence swept over the jubilant worshipers. They could not believe that God would become so angry over a technicality. Why would God smite someone who had acted with the best of intentions? If God reacts with such vengeance, who then can be safe? The response seemed uncalled for.

God was angry, so David responded in kind. "And David became angry because of the Lord's outburst against Uzzah ... so David was afraid of the Lord that day; and he said, 'How can the ark of the Lord come to me?'" (vv. 8-9). So he left the ark there and would not bring it to Jerusalem.

David was not the first man, nor the last, to be angry with

God. Anger is a way of fighting back; it is something we resort to when we feel most hopeless. God has often disappointed us through unanswered prayer and tragic suffering. We resent the fact that we are the victims of some hidden purpose. So we become angry with God as we stand helplessly watching Him do whatever He wills.

Our anger is not necessarily sinful, for God seems to encourage His people to grapple with the tough questions (see Job 18:4; 30:20-21). What we do with our anger, however, is incredibly important. We can learn from David's experience what we should and should not do when we are upset with God. Remembering who God is and who we are will help us when we are tempted to be angry with the Almighty.

God Is Sovereign

God can do as He wishes with His creatures, but we should not think that His actions are arbitrary or capricious. He does not cause us suffering for suffering's sake. There is always a higher purpose, an agenda that has eternal implications.

In this case, David needed to learn that God has the right to expect us to obey His most meticulous commands. David had ignored the divine instructions on how to move the ark of God. The Kohathites (descendants of Levi) were to cover the holy objects, "so that they may not touch the holy objects and die" (Nm 4:15). And again, "But they shall not go in to see the holy objects even for a moment, lest they die" (v. 20). To recap: God had said specifically that: (1) no one should touch the ark nor even glance at it—evidently the veil was to be draped over it when the tabernacle was moved; and, (2) if the ark needed to be carried independently, it was to be carried on the shoulders of the priests, with poles passed through the golden rings attached to it. How much more clearly could God have said it?

What was the ark of God doing on a cart in the first place? This was the way the pagan Philistines had carried it (see 1 Sm 6:7). David and his men should have known that even the priests (Kohathites) were not to glance at the ark, much less touch it.

But did not Uzzah mean well? Were not his intentions beyond reproach? Through this act, God was saying with unmistakable clarity that *no act of disobedience ever has good intentions*. What appeared to be an act of heroism was really a flagrant violation of explicit instructions. As R.C. Sproul says, "It was an act of arrogance, a sin of presumption. Uzzah assumed that his hand was less polluted than the earth. But it wasn't the ground or mud that would desecrate the ark; it was the touch of a man.... God did not want his holy throne touched by that which was contaminated by evil, that which was in rebellion to him ..." (*The Holiness of God,* Tyndale, 1985, 141). In this day of shoddy ideas about God, it is helpful to remind ourselves that we can approach God only in the way in which He specifies.

Now that we see the violation of these commandments, Uzzah's death is more understandable. God was not acting arbitrarily. Uzzah may indeed have been a Kohathite himself, fully instructed in the teachings of how the furniture of the tabernacle was to be carried. Nonetheless, he was guilty. Hans Küng says, "I am not surprised that Uzzah died, but that the rest of us are still alive" (quoted in Sproul, p. 147).

God has the right to make rules and to punish those who disregard them. He has the right to give life and to take it; to prescribe the proper way to approach Him and to slay those who come on their own terms. We are puzzled by God's reaction to disobedience only because we don't understand His holiness. We forget that He is the potter, and we are the clay.

Yet knowing that God is sovereign often only increases our bitterness. We resent the fact that He does not consult us about how He runs His world. We are particularly incensed when we suspect that He brings suffering into our lives just to develop our character and give us greater opportunities to trust Him. He sits in the heavens, we think, and enjoys the suffering we endure on earth.

Job's wife was angry with God. She suggested to her grieving husband that he curse God and die. He correctly replied, "You speak as one of the foolish women speaks. Shall we indeed accept good from God and not accept adversity?" (Job 2:10). Those are the words of a man who had just lost ten children to a windstorm; a man who understood that behind that storm was the will and purpose of God. Job knew that God had the right to run the world as He pleased.

Yes, God is sovereign, but there is more to the story.

We Are Creatures

David's emotions were out of control. "And David was unwilling to move the ark of the Lord into the city of David with him; but David took it aside to the house of Obededom the Gittite" (2 Sm 6:10). David overreacted, saying, in effect, that if that's the way God wanted to treat His people, then he wouldn't move the ark at all. He decided to nurse his anger rather than deal with it.

Remember the story of proud King Nebuchadnezzar in the Book of Daniel? One day this arrogant monarch took a walk on the roof of his royal palace in Babylon. He mused to himself, "Is this not Babylon the great, which I myself have built as a royal residence by the might of my power and for the glory of my majesty?" (Dn 4:30).

Just as he finished the sentence, God spoke to him out of heaven:

> King Nebuchadnezzar, to you it is declared: sovereignty has been removed from you, and you will be driven away from mankind, and your dwelling place will be with the beasts of the field. You will be given grass to eat like cattle, and seven periods of time will pass over you, until you recognize that the Most High is ruler over the realm of mankind, and bestows it on whomever He wishes.
>
> DANIEL 4:31-32

With that the king was driven away and began eating grass like cattle; his hair grew like eagle feathers and his fingernails like birds' claws. But at the end of that experience, Nebuchadnezzar understood who God was; and by definition, he also now understood who he was. His understanding returned to him and he blessed the Most High: "And all the inhabitants of the earth are accounted as nothing, but He does according to His will in the host of heaven and among the inhabitants of the earth; and no one can ward off His hand or say to Him, 'What hast thou done?'" (Dn 4:35).

Yes, we are the clay, He is the potter, but this does not mean that God is indifferent to our plight. Read the Bible and you will find that God has emotions, sensitive emotions, and is constantly responding to our cries. David himself wrote:

> I waited patiently for the Lord; and He inclined to me, and heard my cry. He brought me up out of the pit of destruction, out of the miry clay; and He set my feet upon a rock making my footsteps firm. And He put a new song in my mouth, a song of praise to our God. Many will see and fear, and will trust in the Lord.
>
> PSALM 40:1-3

Resolving Our Anger

When David became angry with God, he forgot that he was the creature and God was the Creator. It's dangerous to think we can reverse roles.

Three months later David heard that the presence of the ark in the house of Obededom was a blessing to those who lived nearby. David interpreted this as a signal that it was time for him to lay his anger aside and get the ark. Somewhere between 2 Samuel 6:10 and verse 12, David had a change of heart.

He also did a bit of research to refresh his memory on how the ark was to be carried (see 1 Chr 15:15). The ark was carried on the shoulders of the Levites, just as God commanded. We also read, "And so it was, that when the bearers of the ark of the Lord had gone six paces, he sacrificed an ox and a fatling" (2 Sm 6:13). David offered the sacrifice to show his repentance for having become so angry against the Lord he loved.

When we are angry with God, we must do the one thing we detest, submit to Him and His authority. *To retain our bitterness is to cut ourselves off from the very help we need.*

How can we best help the abused child who feels betrayed by God? How can we see grace poured into the lives of those who are angry because God did not keep them from a bad marriage or a painful disease? Help is needed, because anger at God is often the root of many spiritual maladies.

First, we must *encourage people to express their anger toward God.* Many people believe that such open confession is sinful., but they must understand that God already sees the heart; there is nothing we can say about our feelings that God does not already know. The greater sin is to be angry at God without being willing to admit the truth about the hostility in our hearts. God knows the pain within, why not tell Him in our own words?

Obviously, I believe we should never lash out at God irreverently, heaping abuse on Him, but to tell Him exactly how we feel is important in taking that first big step toward emotional healing. David spilled out his disappointment with God on numerous occasions.

Read the psalms where David expressed his deep hurt to God and they all have one characteristic: After his doubts and disappointments are verbalized, God pours grace into David's heart. He ends with thanksgiving and rejoicing.

How long, O Lord? Wilt Thou forget me forever? How long wilt Thou hide Thy face from me? How long shall I take counsel in my soul, having sorrow in my heart all the day? How long will my enemy be exalted over me?... But I have trusted in Thy loving-kindness; my heart shall rejoice in Thy salvation. I will sing to the Lord, because He hath dealt bountifully with me.

PSALM 13:1-2, 5-6

Psalm 22 was written to prefigure the suffering of Christ on the cross. But let us not forget that these sufferings were experienced by David first.

My God, my God, why hast Thou forsaken me? Far from my deliverance are the words of my groaning. O my God, I cry by day, but Thou dost not answer; and by night, but I have no rest.... You who fear the Lord, praise Him; all you descendants of Jacob, glorify Him, and stand in awe of Him, all you descendants of Israel. For He has not despised nor abhorred the affliction of the afflicted; neither has He hidden His face from him; but when he cried to Him for help, He heard.

PSALM 22:1-2, 23-24

Second, when we tell God our deepest hurts, and choose to lay down our anger, we are restored. David has sometimes been criticized for "dancing before the Lord with all his might"; but, "David *and all the house of Israel* were bringing up the ark of the Lord with shouting and the sound of the trumpet" (2 Sm 6:15, emphasis added). This was not a sensual dance, but a dance of joy and celebration.

One of David's wives, Michal, the daughter of Saul, was not amused. She thought that her famous husband was acting rather unkingly. As she looked at him through the window, she "despised him in her heart" (v. 16). David explained that he was dancing before the Lord, and in his estimation it was perfectly proper.

Rather than be reconciled on the issue, we read, "And Michal the daughter of Saul had no child to the day of her death" (v. 23). The strong implication is that David, in anger, refused to have sexual relations with her for the rest of their marriage. This was not exactly the kind of sensitive response that one might expect from a man of God, but David was all too human. Though his life was filled with conflict, he found it hard to learn some basic lessons in "conflict resolution."

How do we handle anger toward God? A woman shared this story during an interview on a television program: She grew up an atheist, had attended no church, and had uttered no prayers. At the age of thirty-six, she heard the news that her daughter had been in a serious car accident, and was in a coma that would perhaps last for years. To cope with her anger and grief the woman went to a bar, drank heavily, and got in her car to drive home. Rain was pouring on her windshield as the wipers tried to keep up with the downpour. She pulled to the side of the road, turned off the engine, and began to curse God. For half an hour all the venom of a lifetime spilled out as she finally had the courage to tell God what she thought of Him. When she was finished, there was dead silence. Then she heard a voice:

"This is the first time you have talked to me ... I love you."

Many who are reading these words should stop right now and find a quiet place to reverently and honestly let all the bitterness spill out. Then, like David, they will hear the voice of the Lord.

Talk to Him. He loves you.

Chapter Nine

Conflict With Unanswered Prayer
(Read 2 Samuel 7-8)

Few great men or women live without moments of both elation and disappointment. The president who is praised one day is cursed the next. The successful investor misreads the trends and the brilliant executive gets fired. Life is a series of mountaintops and valleys, and we do not know which one we'll experience tomorrow.

The same chapter that is the high point of David's life also details his struggle with an unfulfilled desire. God denied him the privilege of seeing his most fond wish come true, but in return He loaded him with a series of new promises. This chapter is a picture of one man's intimate relationship with God. As Keith Kaynor says, "The Spirit of God pulls back the curtains, not only to the living room of the palace, but also to the very heart and mind of the king" (*When God Chooses,* Regular Baptist Press, 1989, 201). Here we have a touching portrait of David and his God, one on one.

David had led the nation to a position of prominence and respect throughout the whole region of what we call the Middle East. His enemies, with few exceptions, no longer hassled him—and when they did, he won. The ark had finally been successfully brought to Jerusalem, so David now had time to talk to Nathan the prophet about his heart's desire.

Specifically, David dreamed about building a beautiful temple that would be worthy of the Lord he loved. The ark needed a majestic setting, a place of permanent rest. David said to Nathan the prophet, "See now, I dwell in a house of cedar, but the ark of God dwells within tent curtains" (2 Sm 7:2). The implication? Let me build the temple, an edifice worthy of God.

There were powerful reasons why this was a good desire. First, God wanted it done. He had chosen the city of Jerusalem as the location where the ark should dwell. This was the city that was to bear the name of Jehovah, "For the Lord has chosen Zion; he has desired it for His habitation" (Ps 132:13). Second, David had a good motive. He didn't want to build a monument to himself, but rather he intended to build a monument to God. Third, he had the ability and time to do it. This would be his most exciting challenge.

And why not? Dreams are the engine that keeps us motivated to live productively.

We are all the dreamers of dreams;
On visions our childhood is fed,
And the heart of a child is undaunted, it seems,
By the ghosts of dreams that are dead.

> From "To Dream Again," by William Carruth

The day that David told Nathan about his desire the prophet was enthusiastic. "Go, do all that is in your mind, for the Lord is with you" (2 Sm 7:3). What an encouragement! David was elated! But that night God communicated with Nathan and told him that he had spoken too soon.

In the morning this word arrived from heaven: "Go and say to My servant David, 'Thus says the Lord, "Are you the one who should build Me a house to dwell in? For I have not dwelt in a house since the day I brought up the sons of Israel from Egypt, even to this day; but I have been moving about in a tent, even in a tabernacle""" (vv. 5-6). God implied that He had not yet asked to have a temple built, and for now He was content to dwell in a tent with curtains.

Later David would learn that the real reason he was not allowed to do this project was that he was a man of bloodshed. The Lord said, "You have shed much blood, and have waged great wars; you shall not build a house to My name, because you have shed so much blood on the earth before Me" (1 Chr 22:8). It would not be appropriate for David to build the temple that symbolized peace, worship, and holiness. Whether it seemed reasonable to David or not, God would arrange for the temple to be built by one of David's descendants.

Yet even when He says no, God is sensitive to the desires of His people—especially David, whom He so fervently loved. So the Lord gave him incredible promises as a substitute for the unfulfilled desire. In fact, *though David wanted to do something wonderful for God, God turned the tables and did something wonderful for David.*

Let's notice how God's compassion is shown even though David's specific request was unanswered.

The Gift of New Promises

God began by reminding David of the great personal blessings he had been given: "I have been with you wherever you have gone and have cut off all your enemies from before you; and I will make you a great name, like the names of the great men who are on the earth" (2 Sm 7:9). David's successful past was wholly attributable to God; he could look back with satisfaction, knowing that he had the attention and favor of the divine Shepherd.

Second, God told David that He would give him rest from all of his enemies. The harsh reality of war would fade in the light of God's special protection. The conflict in the kingdom would subside for now.

Third, and most important, the Lord promised that although David would not be allowed to build a house for God, *God would build a house for David!* This house would not be a literal temple, but a lineage, descendants who would sit on Israel's throne and rule over the Promised Land. This house would outlast any earthly building.

The promise had three aspects:

When your days are complete and you lie down with your fathers, I will raise up your descendant after you, who will come forth from you, and I will establish his kingdom. He shall build a house for My name, and I will establish the throne of his kingdom forever. I will be a father to him and he will be a son to Me; when he commits iniquity, I will correct him with the rod of men and the strokes of the sons of men, but My loving-kindness shall

not depart from him, as I took it away from Saul, whom
I removed from before you. And your house and your
kingdom shall endure before Me forever; your throne
shall be established forever.

2 Samuel 7:12-16

The first part of the prediction referred to David's descendant, Solomon, who would build the temple. Naturally, David
was reminded of God's discipline of King Saul, and he might
have wondered whether his son would experience the same
fate. God answered this concern with the assurance, "But My
loving-kindness shall not depart from him, as I took it away
from Saul, whom I removed from before you" (v. 15). God
would not abandon this ruler even if he were disobedient.
David must have breathed a sigh of relief, thankful for the
assurance that God's discipline would not mean the with-
drawal of God's favor.

The second part of this promise had to do with the distant
future: "And your house and your kingdom shall endure
before Me forever; your throne shall be established forever"
(v. 16). Here was the assurance that what David had begun in
Jerusalem would continue without end.

Notice what was included in this promise: Specifically,
David would have a *house,* that is, descendants; a *kingdom,*
which is territory over which the dynasty would rule; and a
throne, which is political power. This covenant was enduring,
for it was established forever.

Three important observations: First, this covenant was
unconditional, that is, it would be fulfilled regardless of the
failures of David's descendants. In Psalm 89 the certainty of its

fulfillment is clear: "I have made a covenant with My chosen; I have sworn to David My servant, I will establish your seed forever, and build up your throne to all generations" (vv. 3-4). And, as if that were not enough, the passage goes on to say that even if David's sons should violate the law of God, they will be disciplined but this will not change the promise: "My covenant I will not violate, nor will I alter the utterance of My lips. Once I have sworn by My holiness; I will not lie to David. His descendants shall endure forever, and his throne as the sun before Me" (vv. 34-36).

A second observation: It appears as though this promise was to be interpreted literally, that is, that David's kingdom would encompass the geographical territory over which David himself ruled. Surely David did not interpret this as a promise to be fulfilled on a throne in heaven, or a spiritual throne in the human heart.

Third, obviously the promise is not being fulfilled today. Not one of David's descendants is ruling over the Promised Land, nor has there been an unbroken line of kings from David to the present. Ultimately, the promise can be fulfilled only by Christ Himself, ruling in the millennial kingdom.

This correlates with what the angel said to Mary when she was told that she would bear the Son of God: "He will be great, and will be called the Son of the Most High; and the Lord God will give Him the throne of His father David; and He will reign over the house of Jacob forever; and His kingdom will have no end" (Lk 1:32-33). The only reasonable way to interpret this is that Christ will someday rule over this earth from the city of Jerusalem, fulfilling the details of the covenant.

God's dream for David makes David's dream for God fade

into insignificance. David wanted to build a temple; God was going to build an everlasting dynasty. David's plans could last only for time; God's would endure for eternity. David was overcome by the goodness of God toward him: "Who am I, O Lord God, and what is my house, that Thou hast brought me this far?" (2 Sm 7:18). Praise for God's mercy and loving-kindness then follows.

About thirty-five years earlier David had been anointed near Bethlehem, unsure as to what it all meant. As the book of his life began to unfold, he saw that each page seemed to be better than the last. God met his needs beyond his wildest dreams.

God says yes to us as often as His purposes allow Him to; but when He does say no, He comforts us with His promises. He does not deny our request without compassion. He reminds us that He will be with us, and will stand with us in our disappointment. He fills the void that the unanswered prayer leaves within our hearts.

New Intimacy

Suppose we have several powerful desires; if the strongest of these is met, we would likely find it bearable to live with the others even if they were unfulfilled. Our greatest need is for God; if we learn to find Him fulfilling, our unfulfilled dreams become bearable. With God we can handle the disappointment of the divine no to our cherished requests.

In *The Weight of Glory*, C.S. Lewis says candidly that it is not wrong for us to desire our own good; in fact, our problem is that our desires are often too weak rather than too strong: "We are half-hearted creatures, fooling about with drink and sex and ambition when infinite joy is offered us, like an ignorant child who wants to go on making mud pies in a slum because he cannot imagine what is meant by the offer of a holiday at the sea. We are far too easily pleased" (Grand Rapids: Eerdmans, 1965, 1-2). God, he says, has infinite fulfillment waiting for us if only we were to see Him as the source of our joy.

"I saw more clearly than ever," writes George Müller, "that the first great and primary business to which I ought to attend every day was to have my soul happy in the Lord" (*Autobiography of George Müller*, compiled by Fred Bergen, J. Nisbet Co., 1906, 152). David would have agreed, for he found intimacy with God a gracious delight. Despite his disappointments he could say, "Thou hast put gladness in my heart, more than when their grain and new wine abound" (Ps 4:7).

David was learning that God can substitute for anything, but nothing can substitute for God. First, David was overwhelmed with God's special blessings. He "sat before the Lord," consciously savoring the fellowship this revelation brought. He contemplated his humble origins and pondered his place in God's prearranged future, "And yet this was insignificant in Thine eyes, O Lord God, for Thou hast spoken also of the house of Thy servant concerning the distant future. And this is the custom of man, O Lord God. And again what more can David say to Thee? For Thou knowest Thy servant, O Lord God!" (2 Sm 7:19-20).

David did not forget his roots, the years spent tending the sheep and running from Saul. He remembered the heartache of Jonathan's death and the failed marriage to Michal. Yet here he was, promoted by God to an enduring honor.

Next, David broke out in a personal prayer of worship that extols God for His loving-kindness and mercy. He admitted that it was because of God's revelation to him that he found the courage to pray this prayer, and he asked that God's name be honored. Read the prayer he offered while sitting before the Lord:

O Lord, for Thy servant's sake, and according to Thine own heart, Thou hast wrought all this greatness, to make known all these great things. O Lord, there is none like Thee, neither is there any God besides Thee, according to all that we have heard with our ears. And what one nation in the earth is like Thy people Israel, whom God went to redeem for Himself as a people, to make Thee a name by great and terrible things, in driving out nations from before Thy people, whom Thou didst redeem out of Egypt? ... And let Thy name be established and magnified forever, saying, "The Lord of hosts is the God of Israel, even a God to Israel; and the house of David Thy servant is established before Thee."

1 CHRONICLES 17:19-21, 24

There are two ways God can make us content. One is by answering our requests, the other is by *making us satisfied with less and showing us Himself.* David learned that our greatest fulfillment is to enjoy a taste of God's incomparable grace.

And there was something else David could do.

A New Project

David was not allowed to build the temple, but he could help make it happen. Yes, if God's promise to David was that he would have a lineage (a house), then David could begin to build that house by instructing his children in the ways of righteousness.

In subsequent chapters we will discover that David failed as a father. And though he did not yet know it, some dark years lay just ahead. The next pages of his biography would be profoundly bitter, though eventually a successor would arise to fulfill God's promises. But David no doubt began to pray, seeking God's will as to who would succeed him on the throne. He recognized that his influence for good or ill would be carried on in the lives of his children.

David was able to help Solomon by preparing for the massive building project. Rather than sulking about God's refusal, David did whatever was in his power. Years later he told an assembly that Solomon was inexperienced, and, "Now with all my ability I have provided for the house of my God the gold for the things of gold, and the silver for the things of silver, and the bronze for the things of bronze, the iron for the things of iron ... and all kinds of precious stones, and alabaster in abundance" (1 Chr 29:2).

David learned that when God says no to one of our desires, He often gives us the opportunity to help someone else fulfill our dream. If you want to be a missionary but cannot go, send someone else in your place. If you cannot have children, you might be able to adopt a child or be a surrogate parent for children of divorce. "God's refusals," says Allan Redpath, "are loaded with immeasurable possibilities of blessing" (*The Making of a Man of God*, Revell, 1962, 171).

Our dream may not be fulfilled in our way. The dream may come about at another time and under a different label. And if we are willing to accept God's will, we might have a part in seeing it come to pass. To dream a good dream may be just as great as to accomplish it.

New Conquests

Despite the fact that God would not let David build the temple, He continued to make him a great conqueror. Offensively, the Lord fought for David and the Philistines were permanently subdued. "David took control of the chief city from the hand of the Philistines" (2 Sm 8:1). He defeated Moab and Zobah (vv. 2-3) and other nations that surrounded the Promised Land. In summary we read, "So David reigned over all Israel; and David administered justice and righteousness for all his people" (v. 15). His kingdom was consolidated, and he was known as a great king.

When we read the details of these accounts, we might be surprised by David's cruelty. But we must remember that he lived in a day when massacres were common and tribes were subdued by these mass killings.

Defensively God was with David as well. Twice we read that "the Lord helped David wherever he went" (vv. 6, 14). God protected him so that, though he led his troops in battle, his life was always preserved.

In sharp contrast to his cruelty with the warring nations, we see a tender side to David in his care for Mephibosheth, the son of Jonathan. This man who was crippled in both his feet had the unexpected pleasure of eating at David's table. This account has often been used as an illustration of God's grace, for Mephibosheth was treated as if he were David's son, with all rights and privileges (see 2 Sm 9).

In all these ways God compensated for David's unmet desire. God's no is not to discourage us, but to goad us into a more intimate relationship with Himself. Unanswered prayer is often an invitation to a more intimate relationship.

Your Unanswered Prayer

What does David's experience teach us about our unanswered prayers, our disappointments with God? First, in the face of our disillusionments, we should begin by recounting God's blessings. God's no should be interpreted in the light of a thousand yeses! Though it was a great honor for David to be an ancestor of Christ, it is an even greater honor for us to be united with Christ as an heir of God and Christ's joint heir.

Someday we shall be promoted to a throne that is far greater than the earthly throne of David. If David sat before the Lord in rapt attention and worship, how much more should we who have been joined to Christ and are destined to reign in glory forever worship Him! In light of such blessings, God's refusal to answer our earthly requests seems small indeed.

Second, let us never forget that the good intentions we are not allowed to fulfill are still precious in God's sight. We have reason to believe that David will eventually receive credit for the temple he desired to build. And at the very end of the Book of Revelation, Christ identifies Himself as "the root and the offspring of David" (Rv 22:16).

Yes, God recognizes a good motive. The apostle Paul seems to imply that believers will not only be rewarded for the money they gave to the work of the Lord, but also for what they would have given if they had had the opportunity. "For if the readiness is present, it is acceptable according to what a man has, not according to what he does not have" (2 Cor 8:12).

Lynn Anderson says, "God does not judge us so much by what we achieve as by whom we adore. To dream good dreams may sometimes be even more important than to accomplish them" (*Finding the Heart to Go On,* Here's Life Publishers, 1991, 112). Only a few people have the privilege of building a temple, but every one of us can learn to worship and thus delight God's heart. "The Lord is the portion of my inheritance and my cup; Thou dost support my lot.... I have set the Lord continually before me; because He is at my right hand, I will not be shaken. Therefore my heart is glad, and my glory rejoices; my flesh also will dwell securely" (Ps 16:5, 8-9).

Fortunately, David was not able to see the next chapter of his life. No matter how glorious these promises were for the distant future, the immediate future would be filled with days of darkness and nights of pain. The next pages in his book would change his life and the life of his family forever. He would wander from the path; and though he would return to God, his children would not.

"Our disappointments," it is said, "are God's appointments."

God said no to David's request, but promised him the gift of His presence and blessings in a distant future.

David would need all of this encouragement, for the noonday was about to turn to darkness.

Chapter Ten

Conflict With Sexual Desires
(Read 2 Samuel 11-12)

David is the last man you might expect to find in such a mess. But there he was, luring a woman to bed and then lying to cover his sin. When that didn't work, he murdered a man to make sure that he would get by with his "secret."

We are sexual creatures who sometimes find it difficult to celebrate our sexuality. If the truth were known, we might be surprised to find how much of our time and energy is invested in sexual fantasies, struggles with lust and temptation. In a world obsessed with sensuality, it is increasingly easy to fall into Satan's trap.

God gives us powerful passions, and expects us to control them as a test of our loyalty. He also wants to display His power in keeping us free from overt sexual sin. Every day the media bombard us with the lie that limiting sex to marriage is too confining, too "unrealistic." Yet as David learned, sexual purity isn't easy but it is right. To succumb to an affair has bitter consequences.

Fighting Goliath was much easier for David than fighting lustful desires. David dodged many a spear thrown by Saul; but this one, ignited by his own sexual desires, went right to his heart. He was about forty-seven years old when he invited

Bathsheba into the palace. In retrospect, it might have been better if he had died at forty-six.

The Steps That Led Down

You know the story: The king was taking a late afternoon nap on the flat roof of his palace. When he awoke, he walked around and "from the roof he saw a woman bathing; and the woman was very beautiful in appearance" (2 Sm 11:2).

The first step? David *saw* a woman. The more he gazed at her the more his sexual desires were awakened. His blood ran hot as his eyes were riveted on her shapely body. He watched her in the glow of the setting sun.

Unfortunately, that is all that David saw. He did not see that some day he would lose four of his sons because of the action he was now contemplating in his heart. He did not see the guilt, the shame, the murder, and the eventual disintegration of his kingdom. He thought he could get by with this bit of pleasure. Besides, if he did not invite her to the palace, he would always wonder what she really was like. He fantasized about conquering this beautiful lady whom he had seen only at a distance. What is more, he believed he could make her feel like a woman, fully satisfied.

There on the rooftop David made a decision that would be difficult to reverse. The easiest time for him to say no to adultery was when he caught his first glimpse of this unsuspecting beauty taking her afternoon bath. How much different his life would have been if he had prayed, "Lord, I thank you for this beautiful woman you have created, and I praise You that You have destined her to be the wife of another man. Bless them in their own marriage, Amen!" Then he should have turned away, thinking of how God had blessed him with many wives of his own.

Every moment David spent gazing at the woman, his desires increased. The likelihood of his walking away became less. When he took that long look at Bathsheba, he was cutting the anchor and setting out on a river whose speed and size was rapidly increasing. Returning to shore was becoming increasingly more difficult. He enjoyed the sensation of being swept away by the euphoria in his body. Unfortunately, he could not see the dangerous rapids that lay ahead.

Dietrich Bonhoeffer, who died a victim of a Nazi concentration camp, penned a booklet entitled *Temptation*, in which he so vividly writes:

> In our members there is a slumbering inclination towards desire which is both sudden and fierce. With irresistible power desire seizes mastery over the flesh. All at once a secret smoldering fire is kindled. The flesh burns and is in flames.... Joy in God is extinguished in us and we seek all of our joy in the creature. At this moment God is quite unreal to us. He loses all reality and only desire for the creature is real.... Satan does not now fill us with a hatred of God but with a forgetfulness of God. (New York: Macmillan Company, 1955, 117)

At the moment David stared at Bathsheba, he did not hate God, he just forgot He was there. Consumed by his passion for the creature, God was blotted out of his mind.

Second, David *sent* messengers to invite her into the palace. I wonder what he said to his servants. What excuse did he use to lure Bathsheba to his bed without their knowing his real intentions? It made little difference, for once a man has decided to commit adultery, telling a lie (whether big or small) is done easily. If we choose to commit a big sin, the lesser ones follow easily behind.

Next, David *took* Bathsheba and lay with her (v. 4). Did Bathsheba give in because of the prestige of being in bed with the king? Did she have genuine affection for David? Did she still love her husband Uriah? We'll never know.

We also don't know whether David thought about the possibility of Bathsheba becoming pregnant. Maybe she assured him that this was a "safe" time; or perhaps David didn't care. Nothing mattered at this moment except the sexual euphoria that filled his body. If David had lived today, he might have thought of using some form of birth control. But in the heat of the moment, even that might have been ignored.

What if Bathsheba had not become pregnant? Perhaps the affair would not have been discovered, Uriah would not have been killed, and David's family and kingdom would have remained intact. David might have "gotten by" with his sin. Yes, if only!

But can we be sure? No, because sin has unpredictable consequences. When we deliberately sin, we just may begin a series of dominoes triggering events that are wildly out of control. No one can confidently suppose that he or she can bridle the effects of sinful actions, for God controls the outcome.

Perhaps Bathsheba, overwhelmed with guilt, would have told her husband; perhaps she would have used the secret to bribe the king; perhaps the servants would have discovered the real reason why Bathsheba was brought into the palace in the first place. Perhaps, perhaps.

What we do know is that Bathsheba became pregnant and told David the news.

The Cover-Up

This casual affair was not as casual as originally planned. A relationship that began with two "consenting adults" ended up involving a third person; a baby was on the way. David decided he had to convince Uriah that the child was his. The king was in a predicament, but though he had lost a game, he was not about to lose the tournament.

Plan A: David asked that Uriah be brought to Jerusalem under the pretext that he was to inform the king about the state of the battle in Rabbah. Were they winning or losing? (see 2 Sm 11:6-7). This would give David an excuse to send Uriah home, so that he would make love to his beautiful wife. David would see to it that a gift accompanied the warrior in the hope that this would foster a romantic spirit and lead the couple to the bedroom.

But Uriah didn't play David's game. We don't know what suspicions (if any) he had. Did he wonder why he was receiving this sudden burst of attention and these privileges? He told David he would not go home, because he would feel guilty if he enjoyed his wife while his comrades were fighting under difficult conditions. "But Uriah slept at the door of the king's house with all the servants of his lord, and did not go down to his house" (v. 9). The king's generous provision was politely refused.

David was desperate. He must get Uriah to go to his house, so that his wife's pregnancy could be explained. After all, this was best for the royal family and for the kingdom.

Plan B: The king asked Uriah to stay another day so that the two of them could eat together. David made him drunk, hoping that in the evening Uriah would go home. But even then this loyal servant stayed with David's servants and simply would not go home to Bathsheba (vv. 12-13). Uriah, it has been said, was a better man drunk than David was sober.

If Uriah had gone home and made love to his wife, would David have been cleared? Bathsheba would have been forced into both living and telling a lie, pretending that the baby belonged to her husband. She would have had to lie to her husband and friends about the premature birth. The child would be a constant reminder of the painful secret that would have had to be guarded with multiple deceptions.

And David would have had to live with the guilt of knowing that he was the father of a child who might later discover his true identity. The king would have to carry this secret in his heart, knowing that his action had precipitated all of these entanglements. Along with the guilt, there would also have been the fear that Bathsheba might tell her husband. What if her guilt simply became too great for her to bear?

Then there was the king's relationship with his wives. What effect would his affair have on them? There was no neat solution to get David out of this predicament.

Plan C: This was David's trump card. He decided to have Uriah killed in battle, so that Bathsheba could become *his* wife. He gave Uriah a letter to take to Joab, his military commander. It read in part, "Place Uriah in the front line of the fiercest battle and withdraw from him, so that he may be struck down and die" (v. 15).

David, how could you!

Why would a good man become a murderer? Why would a good man kill a loyal friend, so loyal that he could be trusted to take his own death warrant to his commander without opening it? Uriah, after all, was one of David's mighty men who had been with him since the days when he was running from Saul. Why, David, we ask, Why? Shame causes us to manipulate the consequences of sin. *By nature we will pay any price to make ourselves look good.*

David would have been better served if he had admitted his sin to Uriah despite the humiliation; then they could have talked about what to do next. The more he covered his sin, the more his sins multiplied. And the greater God's judgment became.

Joab obeyed the king's orders and a messenger returned to tell David that Uriah had been killed. David matter-of-factly replied, "Thus you shall say to Joab, 'Do not let this thing displease you, for the sword devours one as well as another'" (v. 25). In effect he was saying, "That's just the way life is; you win some and you lose some." And with that bit of messy business out of the way, Bathsheba was invited to the palace and she became one of David's many wives.

How well had his cover-up worked? Bathsheba knew the truth; Joab surely knew the truth; David knew the truth; and soon the servants would know, if they didn't already. Most importantly, *God knew the truth!* We read tersely, "But the thing that David had done was evil in the sight of the Lord" (v. 27). The Almighty would see to it that David's cover-ups would soon be uncovered.

Herein lies the irony: We as humans are often more concerned about what *people* know than with what God knows. Yet it is the divine Lawgiver who personally supervises the punishment of those who tamper with His authority. Everything, even our hidden thoughts, are seen by the eyes of God. "And there is no creature hidden from His sight, but all things are open and laid bare to the eyes of Him with whom we have to do" (Heb 4:13).

For perhaps a year or more David played the game, acting as though all was well, adjusting to his guilt as best he could. Bathsheba became his wife and the child was born. David thought he could simply outlive the rumors and wait until the sun would shine again. But a storm was about to break.

David's close friend Nathan, the prophet with whom he had discussed the building of the temple, came to him with a story: A rich man had a traveler stay with him, and instead of killing one of his many sheep he stole the one little lamb that was owned by a poor neighbor. What should be done to the man who would have the audacity to steal a lone sheep, though he had flocks and herds of his own?

David reacted with anger and revenge, "As the Lord lives, surely the man who has done this deserves to die" (2 Sm 12:5). Then his temper cooled and he modified his judgment: "And he must make restitution ... fourfold, because he did this thing and had no compassion" (v. 6).

Nathan responded, "You are the man!"

David had more compassion for this poor man and his

lamb than he did for Uriah, whom he murdered—another proof of how our passions distort our perspectives!

What follows is a moving message from God Himself. The Almighty reminded David how many blessings He had given him—protection from Saul, wives, and the kingdom. So why would David despise the word of the Lord and do evil? David had sinned in the face of incredible grace and numerous blessings.

Because of David's sin, said the Lord, (1) the sword would never depart from his family (he would pay fourfold); (2) though he had committed this sin in secret, his wives would be publicly violated; and, (3) as an immediate judgment, the baby born to Bathsheba would die. All this simply because David had acted in a moment of passion, and committed murder to cover it up.

Let's pause to catch our breath and try to understand how one small sin had resulted in such severe punishment.

The Interpretation

What powerful lessons can we learn from the experience so far? And what sense shall we make of this harsh judgment?

First, anyone can commit sexual sin—the committed Christian just as well as the casual Christian. Ministers, doctors, missionaries—all are susceptible. How the mighty have fallen!

Our passions have awesome power. These desires can exert subtle and dictatorial power over us. Our firmest resolutions collapse in the wake of the euphoria of sexual attraction. Respectable husbands have abandoned their wives; pastors have resigned from effective ministries; wives have walked away from their families—all for the promise of sexual fulfillment. As one Christian put it, "I hate what I'm doing, but I am powerless to do otherwise; there is a part of me that wants out of this relationship, but there is another part of me that doesn't. I think I have made the choice to do my own thing."

If David, who loved God so passionately, could commit sexual sin, it could happen to us all. Many who self-righteously said, "I never would!" must now shamefacedly confess, "I did."

Second, when we commit sexual sin, *God* is the loser. Nathan told David, "However, because by this deed you have given occasion to the enemies of the Lord to blaspheme, the child also that is born to you shall surely die" (2 Sm 12:14). The enemies of the Lord apparently already knew David's "secret," and were saying that he was really no better than they themselves! Just as in our day when a minister commits adultery the reputation of God is tarnished, so David had dishonored the Lord's good name. *God* would live with the fallout.

God could have cooperated in the cover-up; He could have chastened David privately so that His choice servant would not have experienced public humiliation. By nature we do everything we can to hide our sin, but God cannot be counted on to help us. We make plans to cover it; He makes plans to expose it.

David went to great lengths to cover his sin, yet was so unsuccessful that even today people who know little about David know that he committed adultery. The sin he tried to hide is the one for which he is best known. God simply would not be an accomplice to keeping it hidden.

We will probably not be serious about dealing with sexual

sin until we realize how much it grieves God. Nathan, you will recall, asked David why he had despised the word of the Lord in the face of all of God's goodness to him. How could David, who was promised the blessing of a house and lineage—how could he take God's commandments about adultery and murder so lightly? In sexual sin we lose, but so does God.

Was not David's punishment too severe? Was one act of passionate sin and murder deserving of the humiliation of domestic rebellion and the public rape of his wives and concubines? Was it really necessary that four of David's sons eventually die so that Uriah's murder be avenged "fourfold"?

One reason for this strict discipline is that God was judging David by the very words that had come out of his own mouth. He had said that the man who stole the lamb should repay "fourfold." The other reason is that the eyes of the kingdom were on David. A lenient punishment might be interpreted to mean that God makes allowances for His favorites.

Let's also remember that we always reap more than we sow. A single kernel of grain can reproduce itself a hundredfold, but because we also reap *in a different season* than we sow, the effects of our sins are not immediately evident. David's harvest was yet to come.

The Forgiveness

Faced with Nathan's rebuke, David turned to God and experienced the freedom of forgiveness. Though his repentance would not change the judgment God meted out to him, he was freed from a polluted conscience. He and God could be in fellowship, no matter how angry those around him became.

Many people fail to gain this freedom from guilt simply because they confuse the *consequences* of sin with the *forgiveness* of sin. Since the effects of sin continue, they repeatedly take guilt upon themselves even though they have received God's forgiveness. David understood that he could be totally cleansed and forgiven despite the awful pain that his sin would bring to himself, his family, and his kingdom.

All the tears in the world could never restore the purity of Bathsheba; all the regret David could endure would not bring Uriah back to life. Yet for all that, he would again sing the songs of Zion. *His forgiveness would be granted in full view of the terrible repercussions that still lay ahead.*

Psalm 51 records David's prayer of confession, showing how he cast himself on the mercy of God. He no longer saw his sin as affecting only other people, but as profoundly grieving God. "Against Thee, Thee only, I have sinned, and done what is evil in Thy sight" (v. 4). David knew that though he could never ask Uriah for forgiveness, he could still be forgiven—because all sin was really against God. If the supreme Lawgiver of the universe had spoken him clean, he could sing again despite the fact that people in the world still pronounced him guilty.

David accepted cleansing as well as forgiveness: "Wash me thoroughly from my iniquity, and cleanse me from my sin" (v. 2). Forgiveness is what God does outside of us; cleansing is His subjective work within our hearts. Our polluted consciences can be made clean; the memories of our sins no longer have authority over us.

How clean did God make David? Nothing can compare to

the brilliant whiteness of freshly driven snow. Yet David knew that God would do even better. "Wash me" he pleaded, "and I shall be whiter than snow" (v. 7).

As proof of his repentance, David accepted God's discipline. He gave up the struggle to maintain his reputation as king. He was now submissive to God, accepting the words of Nathan, excruciating though they were. *The affliction, like a sheepdog, drove him back into the fold.*

If Psalm 51 is David's prayer of confession, Psalm 32 is his reflection on the contrast between the burden of guilt and the blessing of forgiveness. As for the guilt, he writes, "When I kept silent about my sin, my body wasted away through my groaning all day long. For day and night thy hand was heavy upon me; my vitality was drained away as with the fever heat of summer" (Ps 32:3-4). The guilt affected his body; he felt inner weakness.

Guilt drags a person down and makes him susceptible to various addictions; it leads to the despairing rationalization that, if a sin is committed once, it might just as well be committed again. Guilt brings depression even in those moments when our circumstances are delightful.

In contrast, David describes the blessings of forgiveness. "How blessed is he whose transgression is forgiven, whose sin is covered! How blessed is the man to whom the Lord does not impute iniquity, and in whose spirit there is no deceit" (vv. 1-2). The emotional burden is gone! Like being freed from a fifty-pound weight, the forgiven sinner can walk with a light step. The sun can shine again.

Forgiveness also meant that David would again experience God's leading: "I will instruct you and teach you in the way which you should go; I will counsel you with My eye upon you. Do not be as the horse or as the mule which have no understanding, whose trappings include bit and bridle to hold them in check" (vv. 8-9).

David's point: As long as he was out of fellowship with God, he was totally unaware of divine leading. He was like a horse or mule who refused to return to his owner until forced to do so with a bridle. Yet repentance not only took away David's sin, it brought the presence of God back into his life.

How did David make this transition from guilt to blessing? He gave up his deceit (v. 2). He realized, as all of us must, that we have an endless capacity for self-deception. And nowhere do we deceive ourselves more easily than with the sins of the flesh. David gave up the illusion that his sin was hidden; he faced it in the presence of God and those around him.

Time did not obliterate David's guilt. Nor do drugs or alcohol. No self-inflicted wounds of punishment can pay for our rottenness.

The Good News of Grace

A thousand years later, Christ came to die on the cross as payment for David's sin, and for the sins of us all. This payment was received by God as complete; there is nothing we can add to it. Many Christians falsely assume that they should live with guilt as God's discipline; they don't understand that *the only purpose of guilt is to bring us to repentance.* Once our sin has been confessed, the guilt we continue to experience originates with ourselves or with Satan; it is not of God.

If Christ has made a full payment for my sin, why should I continue to think that bearing my guilt is necessary for complete forgiveness? Does God demand an additional payment? Does my guilt add to the work of Christ? No! A thousand times no!

No man can fall so deep but that God's grace can yet reach him. David committed a great sin because he lost a series of smaller battles. His sin began in the heart, it developed into words, and then he committed the act. But though he had to live with the memory of the man he had killed and the lives he had hurt, he sang a song of forgiveness.

Women who have had abortions, young people caught in the sin of immorality, and addicts who have ruined their families—all can take heart from the experience of David. This is the story of a man who stood with a forgiven heart amid ruins of his own making.

With God's discipline came the grace of divine forgiveness and also the grace of divine providence. In the previous chapter, we learned that God promised David a son who would build the temple and continue the lineage that would eventually bring forth Israel's everlasting king. Who might this be?

The answer is Solomon.

Solomon, born to David by Bathsheba, the wife of Uriah! Solomon, the product of a marriage consummated in adultery and sealed by murder! Solomon, who, strictly speaking, should not have been born! Yet, by God's mysterious grace, he would be the one to inherit the marvelous promises given to his famous father.

Out of the ashes of David's sin God erected a monument to his incredible faithfulness. He would take the mess and make a mosaic that would give hope to millions who have committed similar sins. Even in punishment there would be blessing.

What a message of hope David offers our fallen world.

(Note: Parts of chapter 10 were adapted from Erwin Lutzer, *Living with Your Passions,* Victor Books, 1983, chap. 2.)

Chapter Eleven

Conflict With a Rebellious Son
(Read 2 Samuel 13-18)

Just as the Lord promised, David's name is famous.

We remember him as a great warrior. He not only killed Goliath, but had the courage to lead his men into battle and win many exploits for Israel.

We remember him as a great musician and poet. For three thousand years multiplied generations have been blessed by the psalms in which he shares his many wounds and introduces us to God's healing grace. His broken heart has healed the hearts of millions.

We remember David as a great king. Visit the city of Jerusalem even today and you will see monuments erected to his honor. Jerusalem is, above all, the "City of David."

But we do not remember David as a successful husband and father. It's not just that he sinned with Bathsheba and murdered Uriah, but his sons were undisciplined, disloyal, and rebellious. His wives were unhappy, upset with his favoritism. David could manage his kingdom; he could not manage his family.

Nathan had predicted, "Now therefore, the sword shall never depart from your house.... Behold, I will raise up evil against you from your own household; I will even take your wives before your eyes, and give them to your companion, and he shall lie with your wives in broad daylight" (2 Sm 12:10-11).

Did this mean that the disintegration of David's family was inevitable? Looked at in one way the answer is yes, for God had spoken. But we must also remember that the reason for this judgment was David's sin. And despite his own failures, David could have played a more important role in managing the conflict that developed between the factions of his family.

The Scriptures say nothing about how David treated his sins of murder and adultery within the family context. I think we can assume that he did not confess his sin to his wives and children, asking their forgiveness for his actions. If he had done this, he might have regained enough moral authority to take a firmer hand in his children's misdeeds. As it was, David was a passive father, coping as best he could with murder and treachery without giving either guidance or rebuke to his offspring.

David's sin was forgiven by God, but it paralyzed his family relationships. He lost his moral base and never regained it. Perhaps he thought he did not have the credibility needed to respond to his children in constructive ways. Or maybe he felt awkward, not knowing what he should do. Though he might have had more respect from them than he realized, he became a tragic victim of his own children's rebellion.

When someone asked a worker in an underdeveloped country how he was doing, he replied, "I'm doing far worse than yesterday, but much better than tomorrow!" David would understand that answer. Today was worse than yesterday, but much better than tomorrow would be!

As we read these chapters, we can see David's world

disintegrate. One hammer blow after another threatened to smash his life to pieces. We don't know exactly how long it was after Nathan's rebuke that his predictions came to pass. David's family began to unravel, exposing his failures.

What were David's weaknesses as a father?

He Displayed Anger Without Action

Amnon was David's firstborn son, a child of Ahinoam, one of David's first wives (see 1 Chr 3:2). We don't know whether or not Amnon regarded himself as heir to the throne, because his life was cut short by murder. We do know that he was guilty of a gross sexual crime which left a permanent blot on his record.

Here is the story: Absalom and Tamar, both of whom were unusually beautiful, were children of David's wife Maacah. Amnon became infatuated with his gorgeous half sister, Tamar, and in his frustration almost became physically ill. At the suggestion of a cousin, Amnon devised a plan whereby he would be able to capture Tamar, hoping to talk her into having sex with him (see 2 Sm 13:1-10).

Amnon pretended to be ill; and when Tamar came into his bedroom with food, he asked her, "Come, lie with me, my sister" (v. 11). She refused, telling him that such an act would ruin both of them. If anything, she thought Amnon should ask his father for her and they could be married (she likely made this suggestion to buy some time so she could get away).

Amnon, consumed by lust, would hear none of it, but overpowered her and raped her. Then, in an incredibly pointed commentary about what often happens after illicit sex, we read, "Then Amnon hated her with a very great hatred; for the hatred with which he hated her was greater than the love with which he had loved her. And Amnon said to her, 'Get up, go away'" (v. 15). Lust now turned to disgust. When Tamar wouldn't leave, Amnon had her thrown out of his presence.

Visualize the plight of this violated woman: "And Tamar put ashes on her head, and tore the long-sleeved garment which was on her; and she put her hand on her head and went away, crying aloud as she went" (v. 19). Now sexually stained, she was left to cope with this humiliation as best she could.

What did David do about this act of incest within his own family? We read, "Now when King David heard of all these matters, he was very angry" (v. 21). Then he did what passive fathers always do: *nothing.*

Why did he not rebuke Amnon? Why did he not take Tamar's side in this terrible injustice? Why did he not require that Amnon either ask forgiveness or be put under disciplinary action as required by the law? (see Lv 20:17). Why all this silence?

Two years later, Absalom, Tamar's full brother, worked out a scenario by which he would be able to "even the score." He met his brother Amnon while shearing sheep. Then and there he commanded his servants to kill Amnon, to avenge the mistreatment of his sister (see 2 Sm 13:24-28). They obeyed.

When David heard the news of Amnon's murder, we read, "Then the king arose, tore his clothes and lay on the ground; and all his servants were standing by with clothes torn" (v. 31). Again the king simply chose to live with his anger. He refused to get involved. If he had disciplined Amnon, Absalom might not have felt the urge to kill his half brother in the cause of justice.

David stood by without taking leadership because he was all too aware that they had only committed the sins of their father. Amnon committed a sexual sin; Absalom committed murder. These were the two sins David himself had been guilty of a few years before. Since the elders of Israel had not disciplined him, how could he require it of his son? Now he could only display anger without action.

If you think I am being too harsh in my judgment, consider this inspired comment about David's relationship with another rebellious son, Adonijah: "And his father had never crossed him at any time by asking, 'Why have you done so?'" (1 Kgs 1:6). Little wonder this young man tried to carry out a plot to become king and eventually was murdered at the command of another half brother, Solomon (to be discussed in the next chapter).

For David: *anger, yes; action, no.*

Anger of itself is not wrong or sinful. God Himself often is spoken of as being angry. "God is a righteous judge, and a God who has indignation every day" (Ps 7:11). Paul tells us that when we are angry we should not sin (see Eph 4:26). Unfortunately, when angry, many people either (1) blow up or (2) clam up. Both are counterproductive. Anger should lead us to seek solutions to those issues that raise our ire.

Millions of families today live with passive fathers who are not meaningfully involved in the lives of their wives or children. The mother of the home is often responsible for the discipline and the major decisions of the household. While the children go from one crisis to another, the father is silent.

Guilt, insecurity, and twisted priorities are often the culprits that keep fathers from exercising their God-given responsibilities. And unfortunately, the weakness of the father is often passed on to the children as they cope as best they can with the vacuum left by a father who was emotionally absent.

God does not think that being a passive father is a minor weakness in the life of a man who is otherwise a success. Remember Eli, a man who was by all accounts a faithful, sensitive priest? Yet, though his sons were greedy and immoral, he did nothing about it. Through the lips of Samuel, the judgment of the Lord came to him: "For I have told him that I am about to judge his house forever for the iniquity which he knew, because his sons brought a curse on themselves and he did not rebuke them" (1 Sm 3:13). Remember that when Saul killed all the priests at Nob, this judgment was fulfilled. The massacre took place all because a priest did not rebuke his rebellious sons.

David was paralyzed by his own failures. The powerful king who could subdue pagan armies was helpless as he watched the strife within his own family.

His weaknesses spawned other problems in his family.

Reconciliation Without Forgiveness

After the murder of Amnon, Absalom fled to Geshur, where his mother had lived, and remained there as a fugitive from justice for three years (see 2 Sm 13:37). David mourned for him every day. "And the heart of King David longed to go out to Absalom; for he was comforted concerning Amnon, since he was dead" (v. 39). David was beginning to feel the full effects of Nathan's prophecy; but more heartache was to follow. David was consumed with the desire to see his estranged son, but feared to show softness to him because of his crime. He was caught in a conflict between his duties as a king and his natural instincts as a father. The result was indecision and compromise.

Joab, David's military commander, knew of David's desire to see Absalom and so devised a plan to bring him back. Joab sent a woman from Tekoa to David with a sad story. One of her two sons had slain the other, and the family wanted to put the second boy to death for the murder. This, however, would leave the widowed woman without heirs. The family would be exterminated. David quickly replied (in what appears to have been a breach of justice) that the guilty son should not die.

The woman then applied the parable: The nation was as a widowed mother, Absalom was the single member of the family left, and the king should act in the place of God to bring his banished son home. This parable struck a responsive cord in the aging king's heart.

This analogy was incorrect, since Absalom was not the only heir left in the kingdom, nor should expediency be used to set aside the law. Nevertheless this was the excuse David needed to bring Absalom to Jerusalem. Yet David, once again unsure of himself, decided his son would be placed under "house arrest," and would not be received at the king's palace (14:24).

For two full years Absalom lived in Jerusalem without seeing his father. He was feeling very neglected, so in order to get attention, he had his servants set fire to Joab's grain field. Now that Joab was forced to speak with him, he plainly told the general that he wanted his father to give him full rights. "Why have I come from Geshur? It would be better for me still to be there. Now therefore, let me see the king's face; and if there is iniquity in me, let him put me to death" (v. 32).

Absalom knew that his father would not lay a hand on him. After all, five years had passed since the murder. And since the king was willing to have his son live in Jerusalem, this showed that he was willing to compromise. Boldly, Absalom was asking for full status as a prince without the need to acknowledge any wrongdoing.

Forgiveness was neither requested nor given. The king received his proud and unrepentant son back into full sonship without requiring so much as a single statement of confession. If only David had been as concerned about Absalom's repentance as Nathan had been concerned about *his*. David, when needing to exercise discipline, was needlessly indulgent; when he needed to be forgiving he was often harsh. As already mentioned, he was keenly aware that Absalom's sin resembled his own.

What should David have done? One option would have been to leave Absalom in Geshur until he was willing to return with the heart of the prodigal: "Father, I have sinned against heaven, and in your sight" (Lk 15:18). Or if he did choose to bring him back, he should have confronted his son directly, telling him that unless he was repentant he would not be allowed to stay in Jerusalem. Reconciliation is based on forgiveness.

The seeds of rebellion grew in Absalom's heart because he was restored without displaying a submissive spirit. Since he got by with murder, his greedy heart planned more ambitious conquests. The sins he refused to acknowledge became a launching pad for more serious misdeeds. His ambitions would lead to gross immorality, a plan to kill his father, and eventually to his own untimely death.

David's weakness continued to show.

Sentimentality Without Strength

Now that he was back in the good graces of the king, Absalom used his favor to proclaim himself a judge in Israel. "And Absalom used to rise early and stand beside the way to the gate; and it happened that when any man had a suit to come to the king for judgment, Absalom would call to him and say, 'From what city are you?' And he would say, 'Your servant is from one of the tribes of Israel'" (2 Sm 15:2). Then Absalom would listen to the man's claims and would plant seeds of rebellion by musing how much better it would be if *he* were the king in Israel.

What was the upshot of Absalom's new "ministry"? He gained the following his heart cherished: "So Absalom stole away the hearts of the men of Israel" (v. 6). Under the guise of having a genuine concern for the people, he exploited dissatisfaction within his father's kingdom. Like all rebels, he was not content to let God take care of the kingdom's leadership but plotted to capture power for himself.

After four years, Absalom received permission to go to Hebron to fulfill a vow that he supposedly had made when he was still in Geshur. But this was merely a pretext to send spies throughout all the tribes of Israel, alerting them that when the sound of the trumpet was heard, everyone should proclaim, "Absalom is king in Hebron!" (v. 10).

Here we have the unrepentant heart of a rebel. Like a critical church member, Absalom divided his father's kingdom by refusing to accept his father's anointed leadership. Ambitious hirelings usually operate by: (1) exploiting legitimate needs, (2) pretending that the welfare of the people is first in their minds, and (3) getting people to visualize how much better it would be if they were in charge. When David had fled from Saul, he left by himself; Absalom, who had the heart of a Saul, took others with him.

Humanly speaking, there were reasons for the strength of Absalom's revolt. He himself was attractive, a handsome specimen that attracted the attention of the multitudes. David may have been overworked and therefore may have neglected the legitimate needs of his people. But most importantly, David was under divine discipline for his own sin. Remember Nathan predicted that God would raise up evil against David out of his own house (12:11).

David felt not only the pain of a rebellious son, but also the betrayal of a loyal advisor. Ahithophel, who had befriended the king since his early days, defected to Absalom. Later David would write, "Even my close friend, in whom I trusted, who ate my bread, has lifted up his heel against me" (Ps 41:9). A thousand years later, David's most honored son, the Lord Jesus Christ, would show that Judas was another Ahithophel, who threw loyalty to the wind for some supposed higher gain (see Jn 13:18).

Why would Ahithophel abandon David? Might it not be because he was the grandfather of Bathsheba, and therefore

resented how David had ruined his granddaughter's marriage
and murdered her husband? (Compare 2 Sm 11:3 with 23:34.)
Perhaps his decision to join the conspiracy was the result of
smoldering resentment.

Upon hearing of the rebellion David immediately left
Jerusalem, leaving ten of his concubines behind as a token of
his expected return. Soon he crossed the brook Kidron and
ascended the Mount of Olives. The priests and Levites had left
Jerusalem with the king but returned at David's suggestion
that they could serve him better by remaining in the city and
keeping him posted about developments.

David respected Ahithophel so much that the humiliated
king's prayer was very specific: "O Lord, I pray, make the counsel of Ahithophel foolishness" (v. 31). Then David asked
Hushai, another of his counselors, to return and try to mislead
Absalom (vv. 34-37).

As the procession moved down the valley, Shimei of the
household of Saul ran along the hillside, throwing stones at
David and cursing him as a bloody man. Abishai wanted to kill
Shimei on the spot, but David forbade it. David no doubt
believed that all of these tragedies were happening because of
his sin, and therefore accepted these curses as from God's
hand. He said, "Behold, my son who came out from me seeks
my life; how much more now this Benjamite? Let him alone
and let him curse, for the Lord has told him" (16:11). Even
the cursing of this evil man was interpreted as coming from
the hand of God.

Listen to David's plaintive cry as he fled Jerusalem for his
life: "O Lord, how my adversaries have increased! Many are ris-
ing up against me. Many are saying of my soul, 'there is no

deliverance for him in God.' But Thou, O Lord, art a shield about me, my glory, and the One who lifts my head. I was crying to the Lord with my voice, and He answered me from His holy mountain" (Ps 3:1-4). Finally, as the dawn was breaking, David crossed the Jordan River and at last came to Mahanaim (see 2 Sm 17:24).

Absalom entered Jerusalem, and on the advice of David's turncoat advisor, Ahithophel, had sexual intercourse with his father's concubines on the rooftop—a signal to the nation that there could be no reconciliation between Absalom and David. This was the fulfillment of one more of God's judgments on David (12:11). He had committed adultery secretly; his son did it publicly.

By now the advisor Hushai also arrived in Jerusalem and pretended to side with Absalom. Both counselors were asked for their advice. Ahithophel's suggestion? Take twelve thousand men and attack David immediately while he is still tired. Absalom found this advice favorable. He was ready to leave right away to kill his own father and snatch the kingdom.

But Hushai advised that Absalom should recruit a large army from all of Israel and lead this host into battle personally. Not only David, but all of his followers would be utterly crushed, so as to wipe out all opposition to the new king. This advice was, of course, deliberately deceitful and designed to give David more time to regroup. Absalom accepted Hushai's advice, and Ahithophel was so distraught when his advice was not followed that "he saddled his donkey and arose and went to his home, to his city, and set his house in order, and strangled himself" (17:23).

David was sent word of Absalom's plans and began to organize his resistance. Mahanaim was a strong fortified city, so David was able to devise a strategy to combat the civil war. To his generals he made a personal plea: "Deal gently for my sake with the young man Absalom" (18:5). This request is understandable coming from a father, but it wasn't realistic. After all, this was the young man who had murdered his brother; he had committed immorality with his father's concubines; and now he was leading a massive revolt that would culminate in the deaths of twenty thousand men (18:7). Here was a man who deserved to die along with all those who had instigated the rebellion.

David simply could not bring himself to believe that this son whom he loved so much could be so wicked. He wanted him to have privileged treatment. This decision was based on sentimentality, not on the strength that we would expect from a righteous king. David had killed many others for minor offenses; why should his son be exempt? In fact, God expressly warns parents not to let their feelings of sympathy impact the necessary judgments that a disobedient child should receive: "You shall not yield to him or listen to him; and your eye shall not pity him" (Dt 13:8). Sometimes pity is justice denied.

Absalom went into the battle against his father's army riding on a mule, "and the mule went under the thick branches of a great oak. And his head [hair] caught fast in the oak, so he was left hanging between heaven and earth, while the mule that was under him kept going" (2 Sm 18:9). Though Absalom was still alive he could not extricate himself from the branches. A soldier who saw him told Joab, who became angry with the man for not killing the rebel. The man, however, said that he would not have killed him under any condition, because of the explicit instructions of David.

Joab angrily took three spears in his hand and thrust them through the heart of Absalom. Then he asked ten men to make sure that the rebel was dead. The trumpet was blown and the people knew that the war was over. Absalom was placed in a deep pit in the forest, with a heap of stones over him (vv. 9-18).

David was sitting between two gates when a runner came to tell him news from the front lines. His first question was not whether the battle was going well, but rather whether Absalom was safe. When he was told that Absalom was dead, David began a period of uncontrolled mourning, "And the king was deeply moved and went up to the chamber over the gate and wept. And thus he said as he walked, 'O my son Absalom, my son, my son Absalom! Would I had died instead of you, O Absalom, my son, my son!'" (v. 33).

David was so immersed in his grief that Joab had to eventually reprimand him and bring him to his senses. Of course David's grief was understandable, but his kingly duties required him to be grateful for the victory that his men had achieved. Joab told the king that his uncontrollable grief had covered the faces of his faithful servants with shame. David had loved those who hated him and hated those who loved him (19:6). He owed a word of appreciation to those who had risked their lives for him and his kingdom. "For you have shown today that princes and servants are nothing to you; for I know this day that if Absalom were alive and all of us were dead today, then you would be pleased" (v. 6). David accepted this rebuke as best he could, and made plans for his return to Jerusalem.

For the third time the sword of God had struck in David's family, but this time it pierced directly into his heart. The child born to Bathsheba had died; Amnon was murdered by Absalom; and now Absalom was dead at the hand of Joab. His grief knew no bounds. He cried out to the dead youth, knowing that there could be no answer yet vainly wishing that he had died in his stead.

Father and Son

David stands apart from most other kings because he believed that his kingdom belonged to God. If Saul showed us the heart of a king who believed the kingdom was his, Absalom shows us what it is like to have a subject in a kingdom with the heart of a Saul. The young rebel believed that the kingdom belonged to him, and that he was justified in doing whatever was necessary to secure it.

Gene Edward, in *A Tale of Three Kings,* points out that rebels who ascend the throne by rebellion have no patience with other rebels and their rebellions. When a king with the heart of an Absalom is faced with rebellion by others, he becomes a tyrant. *For those who refuse to be subject to God's anointed authority will be intolerant of those who are not subject to them.* They will eliminate all opposition, because they are obsessed with possessing the kingdom.

Notice, by contrast, David's complete submission to the will and purposes of God. When leaving Jerusalem, the priests accompanied him with the ark, that special chest that David had brought to the city many years before. But David asked them to return to the city and said, "If I find favor in the sight of the Lord, then He will bring me back again, and show me both it and His habitation. But if He should say thus, 'I have no delight in you' behold, here I am, let Him do to me as seems good to Him" (2 Sm 15:25-26).

What a difference between those who believe the kingdom is theirs and those who believe it is God's! "Let Him do to me as seems good to Him" are the words of a man who has been totally broken, completely submissive to the will of God. He would not lift a finger to inherit the kingdom, and he would scarcely lift a finger to keep it.

True, David was drawn into a civil war, and was even willing to go into battle personally to lead his men, though they talked him out of the idea (18:1-5). But even his battle plans were carried out with a feeling of resignation, a feeling that whatever God had planned would be fine with him. Yes, his armies would fight against the armies of Absalom, but he would not resort to personal vindictiveness. He would not defend his kingdom by throwing spears.

The passive father was nonetheless a broken father. God had crushed him and time would be needed for healing.

Chapter Twelve

Conflict on a Deathbed
(Read 2 Samuel 19-24; 1 Kings 1-2)

What epitaph would you like to have on your tombstone? Enoch's was, "He walked with God." Abraham's was "A Friend of God." Saul wrote his own epitaph when he said, "I have played the fool." Christ said of Judas, "It would have been better if he had not been born."

God wrote David's epitaph and recorded it for us. But before we read it, let's summarize the events that took place before he lay on his deathbed preparing to meet the God he loved. Then we will pull back the curtain and watch him die.

We've already learned that David was a failure as a father, and his family was in disarray. The only one of his wives who seemed to command his respect in his closing days was Bathsheba, the woman David dearly loved. She had likely become aware that David had arranged the death of her husband Uriah, and if so, we are surprised that this apparently did not hinder their close relationship. Undoubtedly she had shared Nathan's rebuke, and had repented along with David for her part in the adultery.

We left David on the other side of the Jordan River, where he had fled in response to Absalom's insurrection. We will now describe his return to Jerusalem, and events that unraveled as he prepared to pass from the scene.

Let's look at the clouds that hovered over David in the closing days of his life. This will make the few rays of sunshine all the brighter.

Three Dark Clouds

After Absalom's death, those tribes that had sided with him sent word that they were willing to have David return as king. There was some embarrassment and confusion, because many of the soldiers who had served David for years had sided with Absalom. So David's restoration to the throne depended on a change of heart on the part of these people.

David himself made an overture to the kingdom of Judah, since this had been his home turf. As a gesture of conciliation, he offered to replace his general Joab with Amasa, one of their own number and a man who had actually sided with Absalom (see 2 Sm 19:13).

Eventually, the northern tribes (Israel) also agreed to have David as their king. Thousands came to help him cross the Jordan and bring him back in grand style. Even Shimei, who had cursed him, came begging for forgiveness. In a magnanimous mood, David granted his request. At last he was in the palace in Jerusalem again. But the clouds would not go away.

Cloud #1: If David thought his restoration would be without another embarrassing revolt, he was mistaken. A worthless man by the name of Sheba, of the tribe of Benjamin, blew the trumpet and said, "We have no portion in David, nor do we have inheritance in the son of Jesse; every man to his tents, O

Israel" (20:1). This drew away support for David, as some who had sided with Absalom now had another possible candidate for the kingship.

David continued to be pained by rejection and internal revolt. Again and again he turned to God for the strength to make it through another day, "As for me, I said, 'O Lord, be gracious unto me; heal my soul, for I have sinned against Thee.' My enemies speak evil against me, when will he die, and his name perish?" (Ps 41:4-5). Though David was growing old, the conflicts did not end.

Joab was greatly displeased that he had been replaced by Amasa. So when the king asked Amasa to muster an army to chase Sheba and his supporters, and the new general failed in his assignment, Joab joined along with those who went to quell the rebellion. He also had another item on his agenda.

Amasa, the newly named general, heard that the army was leaving the city without him, so he ran and intercepted them at Gibeon, about six miles north of Jerusalem. There he was met by Joab. Joab approached his successor as if to greet him, but as they came close he stabbed his unsuspecting victim in the abdomen. Amasa lay in a pool of his own blood along the wayside (see 2 Sm 20:10).

Sheba, meanwhile, ran as quickly as he could all the way to Abel, in northern Israel. Joab, pursuing him, laid siege to the city, and the inhabitants expected that all of them might be killed. A woman called to Joab from the wall of the city, urging him not to destroy innocent people. Joab explained that he did not want to hurt the innocent but needed to have the people deliver Sheba to him. Instead, they cut off the head of the traitor and threw it to Joab over the wall (v. 22). This ended the one-man rebellion, but it had cost Amasa his life. The peace of the nation had also been destroyed.

As if this were not enough, God sent a famine to the land for three years—all because of a previous action by King Saul, who had violated Joshua's covenant with the Gibeonites (21:1-2). When David asked the Gibeonites what he could do to avenge Saul's injustice, they asked for seven of Saul's sons to be hanged in Gibeah (four miles north of Jerusalem). David granted their request, but made sure that Mephibosheth was spared. Possibly these seven were chosen because they also were guilty, or had profited from Saul's massacre. At any rate, God's name was vindicated and justice satisfied.

David often remembered the birds that flew so effortlessly in the sky while he herded sheep on the hills of Bethlehem. Now as an old man he wished he were one of them: "O, that I had wings like a dove! I would fly away and be at rest. Behold, I would wander far away, I would lodge in the wilderness. I would hasten to my place of refuge from the stormy wind *and* tempest" (Ps 55:6-8).

But David could not fly away from the conflicts that had dogged him since his anointing at the age of fifteen. Thanks to his disobedience, the entire land of Israel would experience the judgment of God. Even on his deathbed he would be faced with strife within his family and kingdom.

Cloud #2: No sooner had the storm of civil war dissipated than another squall appeared on David's horizon. With his restoration as king firmly in place, he decided to number his fighting men, evidently to assess his strength for military conquests. Once again he was severely disciplined by God.

Because 2 Samuel 21-24 contains a series of appendices that deal with events out of chronological sequence, it has been thought that the numbering of the people may have taken place earlier in David's career. However, it is also probable that it took place after David's return to the city.

For years Bible students have been puzzled over the two accounts of the numbering of the people. In the Samuel account, God is spoken of as the One who brought about this census. "The anger of the Lord burned against Israel, and it incited David against them to say, 'Go, number Israel and Judah'" (24:1). In Chronicles we are told that *Satan* was the one who instigated the numbering. We read, "Then Satan stood up against Israel and moved David to number Israel" (1 Chr 21:1).

Who instigated the numbering? These accounts are not contradictory if we remember that David provoked the Lord with pride, and God responded by allowing Satan to tempt him. Or to put it differently, David fell for Satan's temptation and God used the incident to punish David and the people for their pride. As one writer put it, "God permitted Satan thus to move David, in order that through this act an opportunity might arise for the punishment of Israel's sin" (Keith Taylor, *David King of Israel,* New York: Harper and Brothers, 1875, 371). In the final analysis David knew that he had sinned in ordering the census, and he took responsibility for it.

We aren't sure why this census was displeasing to God. Since it involved counting men who drew the sword (see 2 Sm 24:9), this may indicate that David was planning conquests outside of God's will. Even Joab sensed the danger and asked the king, "Are they not all my lord's servants?" (1 Chr 21:3). As soon as the census was completed, David began to feel uneasy; and

God spoke to him about the coming punishment.

David was given three alternatives, any one of which would weaken the nation. The options were: (1) seven years of famine, (2) three months of military defeat or, (3) three days of plague (see 2 Sm 24:10-14). This may confirm our suspicion that the king and the nation were beginning to depend for their security on their size and military might. God wanted to weaken them so that they would depend wholly on him and not their own strength.

David left the choice to God. The Lord sent pestilence, and soon news of dying people flooded the capital. Knowing that the disease would last three days, there was little to be done except wait until it was over. David toured the land, and when he returned to the city he saw an avenging angel poised over Jerusalem. David fell on his knees and interceded for the people. He not only confessed his sin but also pleaded for his dying people. He asked God to punish him instead. God graciously shortened the plague, though a total of seventy thousand men from Dan to Beersheba died (v. 15).

At the command of the Prophet Gad, David reared an altar to the Lord at the spot where an angel had withheld the plague—which happened to be at a threshing floor. The owner of the threshing floor offered to give it to David but David refused, saying he did not want to give to God what had cost him nothing. Many believe that this spot was the very place where Abraham had been ready to offer up Isaac (see Gn 22), and where the temple of Solomon was later built. On this sacred spot God stopped the hand of judgment as the patriarch raised his knife to slay his beloved son; here in David's day the hand of judgment was again halted as the angel of death was about to destroy Jerusalem; and after the temple had been built, it was here that sacrifices were offered to cover the sins of the people until the perfect sacrifice would come and die for the sins of the world.

Cloud #3: The plague ended, but David's trials were not over. God let David live to see one more act of rebellion within his own family. This was the last conflict David would ever witness, the last storm he would have to endure.

Adonijah, David's oldest son, decided to make a calculated grasp for the throne. David had not yet named a successor, so Adonijah hired a team of attendants and chariots to enhance his credibility for the high office. Why should he wait for his father to die? If you don't elbow your way into leadership, someone else will.

Joab, feeling the sting of rejection by David, decided to participate in the plot of this would-be king. Even Abiathar the priest, who had been with David since the cave of Adullum, decided to back Adonijah in this quest for power. With such backing, Adonijah thought he had it made (see 1 Kgs 1:5).

Meanwhile Bathsheba and a majority of David's mighty men favored Solomon. This young man seemed to be the only bright light among David's children. When he was born we read, "Now the Lord loved him" (2 Sm 12:24). When David heard what his son Adonijah was doing, he called Zadok the priest to his bedside and gave him the order, "Take with you the servants of your lord, and have my son Solomon ride on my own mule, and bring him down to Gihon. And let Zadok the priest and Nathan the prophet anoint him there as king over Israel, and blow the trumpet and say, 'Long live King Solomon'" (1 Kgs 1:33-34). So Solomon was crowned, and there was now no doubt as to who the next king would be. A parade followed and the cheering people ignited support for Solomon as king. When the shout, "God save the king!" rang throughout the city, support for Adonijah began to melt away. Solomon was invited to take up residence in the palace.

Adonijah knew that he was in trouble, so he ran to the altar in the tabernacle for asylum. Solomon had him brought out with the promise that if he behaved himself he would not be put to death. But after David died, Adonijah made a request that he be able to have Abishag the Shunammite as a wife. Since this woman was a part of David's harem, Solomon interpreted this as a veiled move to secure the kingdom and had his brother executed (2:19-25). Life was cruel in those days!

David had now paid for his sin fourfold. *First,* the child that Bathsheba bore died; *second,* Amnon was killed by Absalom in revenge for having raped Absalom's sister Tamar; *third,* Absalom himself was killed in his revolt; *fourth,* David's son Adonijah made a move that cost him his life. What a harvest David reaped for his disobedience!

We've spoken about the darkness, now let us see light. Behind the clouds the sun continued to shine.

The Sunshine

Though David had often failed, he did not die a failure. He maintained his fellowship with God to the end. Indeed, David's last words were filled with praise and hope:

The Spirit of the Lord spoke by me, and his word was on my tongue. The God of Israel said, the Rock of Israel spoke to me, "He who rules over men righteously, who rules in the fear of God, is as the light of the morning when the sun rises, a morning without clouds, when the tender grass springs out of the earth, through sunshine after rain." Truly is not my house so with God? For He has made an everlasting covenant with me, ordered in all things, and secured; for all my salvation and all my desire, will He not indeed make it grow!

2 SAMUEL 23:2-5

In his closing hours David charged Solomon with his responsibilities, and urged him to build the temple to honor God and to lead the people in worship. "As for you, my son Solomon, know the God of your father, and serve Him with a whole heart and a willing mind; for the Lord searches all hearts, and understands every intent of the thoughts. If you seek Him, He will let you find Him; but if you forsake Him, He will reject you forever" (1 Chr 28:9).

Yes, David had many clouds in his forty-year reign in Israel, but even on his deathbed the sun was shining. For through all the ups and downs, through his victories and his sins, through his strength and weakness, *God was there making the sun penetrate the darkness.*

The attendants of the court stole through the hallway silently lest they disturb the aged king. In a few days he would be gone; the nation would mourn, and Solomon would be on his own. God and God alone would have to continue in faithfulness, fulfilling the long-ranging promises made so many years before.

To paraphrase the words on an observatory in Pittsburgh, "David loved the stars too fondly to be afraid of the night."

Then David, with his God, slipped into the night.

Home at Last

David was finally fulfilled as his soul took its flight to God. On earth he had craved for more of the Almighty. "O God, thou art my God; I shall seek Thee earnestly; my soul thirsts for Thee, my flesh yearns for Thee, in a dry and weary land where there is no water" (Ps 63:1). Now at last David's longings were fully satisfied. "In Thy presence is fulness of joy; in Thy right hand there are pleasures forever" (16:11).

What made David so special to God? Why is he even now honored so highly? Despite his failures we always get the impression that *he and God had something special between them.* He had the courage to share his heart with us, and as we read the psalms we know that someone else has walked a painful path to show us the way to God.

Just as flowers don't share their fragrance unless they are crushed, so David would never have blessed the world if his life had been free of conflict. When he was humiliated by his own son's rebellion, he left us an example of what it means to commit our circumstances to God. "Let the Lord do as seems good to Him," he said to those who wanted to accompany him out of Jerusalem.

On his deathbed, David now looked at life through the lens of a broken and submissive man. Though much of what he had worked to accomplish was coming apart, he was still walking with his God. By one standard he would die a failure, but God would judge him by another yardstick, putting the measuring tape around his heart, not his head.

To understand David's end we must remember how he began. In the hills of Judah he first learned that sheep don't have to do anything to be accepted by the shepherd. They just have to be sheep. The more obedient they are to the shepherd, the better for them, because he watches and cares for them. But even when they are rebellious, a shepherd never abandons them. A shepherd is responsible for his sheep, come what may.

Visualize David sitting on a hilltop in the sunset years of life and writing, "The Lord is my Shepherd; I shall not want. He maketh me to lie down in green pastures; He leadeth me beside the still waters."

We want to interrupt him and say, "David, that sounds great, but the sun is shining, the water is cool, the grass is green, God is in heaven, and everything is right with the world. But David, what do you do when Saul attempts to kill you and your best friend dies in battle? What happens when you go into enemy territory and act like a madman to protect yourself? What about times when you take the wrong path?"

He continues, "He restoreth my soul; He leadeth me in the paths of righteousness for His name's sake."

We want to say, "But David, what about the sorrow that comes when a prophet gives you a message of judgment? What do you do when your infant son dies? When you encounter murder and incest in your own family, what do you do? When your rebellious son is hung by his hair and murdered, where will your Shepherd be then?"

He continues, "Yea, though I walk through the valley of the shadow of death, I will fear no evil: for Thou art with me; Thy rod and Thy staff they comfort me."

"But David, what do you do when you're hunted by Saul, and when your trusted advisors suddenly follow a rival king? What do you do when you are chased like a dog through the Kidron Valley by your own son? What do you do when your own wives are publicly humiliated in clear view of the citizens of Jerusalem? Just look at your family! Only one of your sons appears worthy of the throne. Look at your kingdom! It is falling apart. Think of your wives, David, and what they think of you."

He replies, "Thou preparest a table before me in the presence of mine enemies; my cup runneth over."

"But David, what right do you have to think that God will bless you? You have taken God's laws and torn them to shreds; you have taken His commandments and trodden them underfoot; you have failed as a husband and a father ... and now you are dying. How can you expect God to bless you?"

He replies, "Surely goodness and mercy shall follow me all the days of my life, and I will dwell in the house of the Lord for ever." (This dialogue with David is adapted from Norman Archer's book, *David*, Christian Herald Books, 1980, 142–43.)

We're glad that David wrote Psalm 23 for parents who have children that rebel; for discouraged people who come to the end of wasted lives; for those of us who have experienced the sharp pain of disloyalty—all can take heart knowing that David has been through it all, and God was with him all the way. Generations to come will say that they do not want David's failures, but they do want his God.

And so the curtain closes just as it opened: *All there is, is*

David and his Lord. A sheep and his Shepherd.

David knew that dark clouds do not obscure the sun for those who believe. "For with Thee is the fountain of life; In Thy light we see light" (Ps 36:9).

And what is David's epitaph? Hear it from the Lord himself. "David My servant " (89:3).

A shepherd boy from the hills of Bethlehem could not have asked for more.

Epilogue

Centuries pass and a Child is born in Bethlehem, a town known as "the City of David." The Child would grow to become a man and is identified as "the son of David." This man will be both David's son and David's Lord!

Christ used His ancestral relationship with David to puzzle the Jews, who were hopelessly unclear about the coming Messiah. Think through this clever bit of logic:

"What do you think about the Christ, whose son is He?" They said to Him, "The son of David." He said to them, "Then how does David in the Spirit call Him 'Lord,' saying, 'The Lord said to my lord, "Sit at My right hand, until I put thine enemies beneath Thy feet?""

MATTHEW 22:42-44

Then comes Christ's punch-line: "If David then calls Him 'Lord,' how is He his son?" (v. 45).

Dead silence. They simply could not understand how Christ was both David's son and David's Lord. Both man and God!

For all of David's failures, Christ is not embarrassed to be identified with this flawed but famous king. One of the last descriptions of our Lord given in the Scriptures is, "I am the root and the offspring of David, the bright morning star" (Rv 22:16).

The first phase of God's promises to David has been fulfilled. Solomon was born and built a temple for God. A thousand years later a divine King was born as King of the earth. But we still await the fulfillment of the second phase of God's covenant. This King, David's greater Son, will yet rule from Jerusalem:

> And many peoples will come and say, "Come, let us go up to the mountain of the Lord, to the house of the God of Jacob; that He may teach us concerning His ways, and that we may walk in His paths." For the law will go forth from Zion, and the Word of the Lord from Jerusalem. And He will judge between the nations, and will render decisions for many peoples; and they will hammer their swords into plowshares, and their spears into pruning hooks. Nation will not lift up sword against nation, and never again will they learn war.
>
> ISAIAH 2:3-4

When David's Son rules, the hills of Bethlehem become the mountains of the Lord. Of His kingdom there shall be no end.